HEINEMANN POETRY BOOKSHELF

Keats

Selected Poems and Letters

Selected by Robert Gittings

Edited by Sandra Anstey

Series Editor: Andrew Whittle
Series Consultant: Virginia Graham

Heinemann Educational Publishers
Halley Court, Jordan Hill, Oxford OX2 8EJ
a division of Reed Educational & Professional Publishing Ltd

MELBOURNE   AUCKLAND
FLORENCE   PRAGUE   MADRID   ATHENS
SINGAPORE   TOKYO   SAO PAULO
CHICAGO   PORTSMOUTH (NH)   MEXICO
IBADAN   GABORONE   JOHANNESBURG
KAMPALA   NAIROBI

Selected Poems and Letters of Keats first published in Poetry Bookshelf 1966.
This edition first published 1995.
The publishers and Series Editor are indebted to James Reeves for his work as
Founding Editor of the original Poetry Bookshelf series.

10 9 8 7 6 5 4 3
99 98 97

A catalogue record for this book is available from the British Library on request.
ISBN 0 435 15077 4

Cover design by The Point

Text design by Roger Davies

Typeset by Books Unlimited (Nottm)

Printed by Clays Ltd, St Ives plc

CONTENTS

Introduction   vi

Poems and Letters

Critical Approaches

Explorations and Essays

INTRODUCTION

John Keats was only 25 years old when he died, but, during his short life (1795–1821) his achievement as a poet and letter-writer is remarkable. He wrote with great energy and produced work which continues to intrigue and challenge the reader.

Keats, along with other leading writers of his day – Blake, Byron, Coleridge and Shelley – is associated with the Romantic movement which transformed the arts in Europe in the late eighteenth and early nineteenth centuries. The application of the word 'romantic' has, of course, changed over the years. The word which we now use to refer to a love story for example, as in the phrase 'romantic novel', was used in the eighteenth century as a literary term to denote the culture of the Middle Ages and Renaissance. Keats and his contemporaries were not conscious of being members of a recognizable literary group entitled the Romantics. Indeed, it was not until the 1860s that the term was used, with hindsight, as a collective name for the group. These writers were, however, politically in sympathy with the contemporary revolutions across Europe and elsewhere; they also shared a deep concern for personal experience and a belief in the importance of the imagination – all of which placed them in direct contrast to the literature of the early eighteenth century. (You will find more about Keats's life and times on pages 274–7.)

During Keats's lifetime, three volumes of his poetry were published:
Poems (1817)
Endymion (1818)
Lamia, Isabella, The Eve of St Agnes and Other Poems (1820)
Many other poems remained unpublished until after Keats's death.

This new edition of Keats's poems and letters uses Robert Gittings' chronological selection of material (first published in 1966) as its starting-point, and continues the practice of including brackets to indicate dates and words added to make the text of the letters intelligible. Keats's punctuation and spelling (somewhat erratic on occasions) are reproduced in the letters. That 1966 selection, which forms a record of Keats's life and progress in poetry and in prose, appears here with new material to support your study of Keats's writings.

Notes, approaches and explorations

In this edition you will find glossary notes on pages opposite the text for ease of reference, together with points to help you think about the poems and develop your own personal responses.

In the **Critical Approaches** section you will find information about Keats's life, writing, poetic form, themes and ideas. The **Explorations and Essays** section contains activities to help you explore the ideas discussed in **Critical Approaches** and questions for extended writing. Finally, you will find **Writing an Essay about Poetry** and **A Note from a Chief Examiner** useful in helping you prepare for extended coursework assignments and examinations.

I stood tip-toe upon a little hill

This passage is from a much longer poem (242 lines) which Keats left untitled in his first published volume, **Poems** (1817). In the lines printed here the focus is on a stream near his old school in north London.

67   *sallows* – willow trees.

82   *tresses* – long shoots of undergrowth.

Extract from
I stood tip-toe upon a little hill

LINGER awhile upon some bending planks
That lean against a streamlet's rushy banks,
And watch intently Nature's gentle doings:
They will be found softer than ring-dove's cooings.
65 How silent comes the water round that bend;
Not the minutest whisper does it send
To the o'er hanging sallows: blades of grass
Slowly across the chequer'd shadows pass.
Why, you might read two sonnets, ere they reach
70 To where the hurrying freshnesses aye preach
A natural sermon o'er their pebbly beds;
Where swarms of minnows show their little heads,
Staying their wavy bodies 'gainst the streams,
To taste the luxury of sunny beams
75 Temper'd with coolness. How they ever wrestle
With their own sweet delight, and ever nestle
Their silver bellies on the pebbly sand.
If you but scantily hold out the hand,
That very instant not one will remain;
80 But turn your eye, and they are there again.
The ripples seem right glad to reach those cresses,
And cool themselves among the em'rald tresses;
The while they cool themselves, they freshness give,
And moisture, that the bowery green may live:
85 So keeping up an interchange of favours,
Like good men in the truth of their behaviours.
Sometimes goldfinches one by one will drop
From low hung branches: little space they stop;

90   *freak* – change of mind, random impulse.

> This poem has been praised for its exactness of description. Which lines would you select to support this point of view? Give reasons for your choice.

To Charles Cowden Clarke, 9 October 1816

Charles Cowden Clarke was the son of the headmaster at the north London school which Keats attended until 1811.

3   *Hunt* – Leigh Hunt (1784–1859) was a great admirer of Keats, whose poems he printed in **The Examiner** and **The Indicator**.

4–5   *Author of the Sonnet to the Sun* – probably Charles Clarke himself, but possibly a reference to Horace Smith, a contributor to **The Examiner**.

7   *Darwin* – Erasmus Darwin, physician and poet.

10   *those to G Mathew* – a reference to Keats's *Epistle to George Felton Mathew*, addressed to a contemporary who was himself a poet.

21   *a Meeting* – a Baptist chapel.

But sip, and twitter, and their feathers sleek;
90 Then off at once, as in a wanton freak:
Or perhaps, to show their black, and golden wings,
Pausing upon their yellow flutterings.

To CHARLES COWDEN CLARKE
Wednesday 9 Oct. [1816]
My dear Sir,

The busy time has just gone by, and I can now devote any time
you may mention to the pleasure of seeing Mr Hunt—'t will be an
Era in my existence—I am anxious too to see the Author of the
5 Sonnet to the Sun, for it is no mean gratification to become acquainted with Men who in their admiration of Poetry do not jum-
ble together Shakespeare and Darwin—I have coppied out a sheet
or two of Verses which I composed some time ago, and find
                                                                worst
so much to blame in them that the best part will go into the fire—
10 those to G. Mathew I will suffer to meet the eye of Mr H. not
withstanding that the Muse is so frequently mentioned. I here
sinned in the face of Heaven even while rememb[e]ring what, I
think, Horace says, "never presume to make a God appear but for
an Action worthy of a God. From a few Words of yours when
15 last I saw you, I have no doubt but that you have something in
your Portfolio which I should by rights see—I will put you in Mind
of it—Although the Borough is a beastly place in dirt, turnings
and windings; yet No 8 Dean Street is not difficult to find; and if
you would run the Gauntlet over London Bridge, take the first
20 turning to the left and then the first to the right and moreover
knock at my door which is nearly opposite a Meeting, you would
do one a Charity which as St Paul saith is the father of all the
Virtues—At all events let me hear from you soon—I say at all
events not expecting the Gout in your fingers—

Your's Sincerely
John Keats—

On First Looking into Chapman's Homer

This sonnet (see **Critical Approaches** page 279) was written in October 1816 after Keats had read, for the first time, a translation by George Chapman of Homer's *Iliad* and *Odyssey*.

4 *fealty* – loyalty, as between tenant and feudal lord.

4 *Apollo* – Greek god of poetry and music.

6 *demesne* – territory.

7 *serene* – clear air.

10 *ken* – knowledge or perception.

11 *Cortez* – Hernando Cortez, a Spanish explorer. It was in fact Balboa who discovered the Pacific in 1513.

14 *Darien* – an isthmus in Central America.

> *Many critics have pointed to ways in which the vocabulary that Keats uses here differs from what appears in the earlier I stood tip-toe upon a little hill. What differences can you see?*

> *How does the tone change through this poem?*

Keen, fitful gusts

This sonnet makes reference to Keats's visits to Leigh Hunt's cottage in Hampstead where the two discussed, among other things, the poems of Milton and Petrarch.

On first looking into Chapman's Homer

MUCH have I travell'd in the realms of gold,
    And many goodly states and kingdoms seen;
    Round many western islands have I been
Which bards in fealty to Apollo hold.
5 Oft of one wide expanse had I been told
    That deep-brow'd Homer ruled as his demesne;
    Yet did I never breathe its pure serene
Till I heard Chapman speak out loud and bold:
Then felt I like some watcher of the skies
10 When a new planet swims into his ken;
    Or like stout Cortez when with eagle eyes
    He star'd at the Pacific—and all his men
Look'd at each other with a wild surmise—
    Silent, upon a peak in Darien.

Keen, fitful gusts

KEEN, fitful gusts are whisp'ring here and there
    Among the bushes half leafless, and dry;
    The stars look very cold about the sky,
And I have many miles on foot to fare.
5 Yet feel I little of the cool bleak air,
    Or of the dead leaves rustling drearily,
    Or of those silver lamps that burn on high,
Or of the distance from home's pleasant lair:
For I am brimfull of the friendliness
10 That in a little cottage I have found;

12   *Lycid* – a reference to Milton's *Lycidas,* an elegy on the death of a friend who drowned.

13   *Laura* – the subject of a number of love poems by Petrarch.

14   *Petrarch* – Francesco Petrarca (1304–74), Italian poet and scholar.

As you read the sonnet, note the way in which the tone changes as the poem progresses. How does this shift in tone link with the structure of this sonnet?

To my Brothers

This sonnet was written in November 1816 on the birthday of Thomas Keats, John's younger brother. At that time the three brothers were living together in London.

3   *household gods* – the *lares et penates,* the Roman gods of the hearth who were guardians of the home.

7   *lore* – learning.

7   *voluble* – changeable, fluent.

8   *condoles* – offers sympathy or comfort.

How would you describe the tone of this sonnet? Select words and phrases from the poem to support your view.

To Haydon

This sonnet, written in November 1816, is addressed to Benjamin Robert Haydon, a painter whom Keats had met earlier that year.

1   *sojourning* – staying.

2   *He of the cloud* – William Wordsworth who lived in Cumbria, in sight of the mountain, Helvellyn.

4   *Archangel* – an angel of the higest order.

5   *He of the rose* – Leight Hunt who, during a time in prison, transformed his cell into a rose bower using appropriate wallpaper.

Of fair-hair'd Milton's eloquent distress,
    And all his love for gentle Lycid drown'd;
Of lovely Laura in her light green dress,
    And faithful Petrarch gloriously crown'd.

To my Brothers

SMALL, busy flames play through the fresh laid coals,
    And their faint cracklings o'er our silence creep
    Like whispers of the household gods that keep
A gentle empire o'er fraternal souls.
5   And while, for rhymes, I search around the poles,
    Your eyes are fix'd, as in poetic sleep,
    Upon the lore so voluble and deep,
That aye at fall of night our care condoles.
This is your birth-day Tom, and I rejoice
10   That thus it passes smoothly, quietly.
Many such eves of gently whisp'ring noise
    May we together pass, and calmly try
What are this world's true joys,—ere the great voice,
    From its fair face, shall bid our spirits fly.

To Haydon

GREAT spirits now on earth are sojourning;
    He of the cloud, the cataract, the lake,
    Who on Helvellyn's summit, wide awake,
Catches his freshness from Archangel's wing:
5   He of the rose, the violet, the spring,
    The social smile, the chain for Freedom's sake:
    And lo!—whose stedfastness would never take

8   *Raphael* – an archangel, also the name of a famous Renaissance painter. Both references are a tribute to Haydon.

> *What ideas are being explored in the closing lines of the poem?*

> *Line 13 was originally completed with the words 'in a distant Mart'. What effect does the incomplete line have on your reading of the poem?*

On the Grasshopper and Cricket

This poem was written in December 1816, as the consequence of a competition between Keats and his friend Leigh Hunt to write a sonnet on a set subject in a set time.

> *What idea is Keats exploring in this poem? Which phrases emphasize his thoughts?*

> *Discuss with a partner or group any features you note about the structure of the sonnet.*

> *What effect does the repetition in the opening of lines 1 and 9 have on your understanding of the poem?*

To John Hamilton Reynolds, 17 April 1817

This letter was written from the Isle of Wight where Keats planned to finish writing *Endymion*. For the first time in his adult life he was on his own and away from London. John Hamilton Reynolds was an author, critic and lawyer who befriended Keats in 1816.

5   *Haydon* – Benjamin Haydon (1786–1846) was a painter of portraits and topical scenes. Keats had taken a drawing by Haydon with him to the Isle of Wight.

A meaner sound than Raphael's whispering.
And other spirits there are standing apart
10   Upon the forehead of the age to come;
These, these will give the world another heart,
    And other pulses. Hear ye not the hum
Of mighty workings?—
    Listen awhile ye nations, and be dumb.

On the Grasshopper and Cricket

THE poetry of earth is never dead:
    When all the birds are faint with the hot sun,
    And hide in cooling trees, a voice will run
From hedge to hedge about the new-mown mead;
5   That is the Grasshopper's—he takes the lead
    In summer luxury,—he has never done
    With his delights; for when tired out with fun
He rests at ease beneath some pleasant weed.
The poetry of earth is ceasing never:
10   On a lone winter evening, when the frost
    Has wrought a silence, from the stove there shrills
The Cricket's song, in warmth increasing ever,
    And seems to one in drowsiness half lost,
    The Grasshopper's among some grassy hills.

To JOHN HAMILTON REYNOLDS
Thursday 17 April [1817]

Carisbrooke April 17th

My dear Reynolds,

Ever since I wrote to my Brothers from Southampton I have been in a taking, and at this moment I am about to become settled for I have unpacked my books, put them into a snug corner—
5   pinned up Haydon—Mary Queen [of] Scotts, and Milton with his daughters in a row. In the passage I found a head of Shakespeare

28 *quick freshes* – *The Tempest*, Act 3, scene 2, 77.

42 *Barracks* – built on the Isle of Wight during the Napolenonic Wars as a base for recruits.

which I had not before seen—It is most likely the same that George
spoke so well of; for I like it extremely—Well—this head I have
hung over my Books, just above the three in a row, having first
10 discarded a french Ambassador—Now this alone is a good morning's work. Yesterday I went to Shanklin, which occasioned a great
debate in my mind whether I should live there or at Carisbrooke.
Shanklin is a most beautiful place—sloping wood and meadow
ground reaches round the Chine, which is a cleft between the Cliffs
15 of the depth of nearly 300 feet at least. This cleft is filled with trees
& bushes in the narrow part; and as it widens becomes bare, if it
were not for primroses on one side, which spread to the very verge
of the Sea, and some fishermen's huts on the other, perched mid-
way in the Ballustrades of beautiful green Hedges along their steps
20 down to the sands.—But the sea, Jack, the sea—the little waterfall—then the white cliff—then St. Catherine's Hill—"the sheep in
the meadows, the cows in the corn."—Then, why are you at Carisbrooke? say you—Because, in the first place, I sho^d be at twice the
Expense, and three times the inconvenience—next that from here
25 I can see your continent—from a little hill close by, the whole north
Angle of the Isle of Wight, with the water between us. In the 3^d
place, I see Carisbrooke Castle from my window, and have found
several delightful wood-alleys, and copses, and quick freshes—As
for Primroses—the Island ought to be called Primrose Island: that
30 is, if the nation of Cowslips agree thereto, of which there are diverse Clans just beginning to lift up their heads and if an how the
Rain holds whereby that is Birds eyes abate—another reason of my
fixing is that I am more in reach of the places around me—I intend
to walk over the island east—West—North South—I have not seen
35 many specimens of Ruins—I dont think however I shall ever see
one to surpass Carisbrooke Castle. The trench is o'ergrown with
the smoothest turf, and the Walls with ivy—The Keep within side
is one Bower of ivy—a Colony of Jackdaws have been there many
years—I dare say I have seen many a descendant of some old
40 cawer who peeped through the Bars at Charles the first, when he
was there in Confinement. On the road from Cowes to Newport I
saw some extensive Barracks which disgusted me extremely with

Government for placing such a Nest of Debauchery in so beautiful a place—I asked a man on the Coach about this—and he said that
45 the people had been spoiled—In the room where I slept at Newport I found this on the Window "O Isle spoilt by the Milatary!"—I must in honesty however confess that I did not feel very sorry at the idea of the Women being a little profligate—The Wind is in a sulky fit, and I feel that it would be no bad thing to be the favorite
50 of some Fairy, who would give one the power of seeing how our Friends got on, at a Distance—I should like, of all Loves, a sketch of you and Tom and George in ink which Haydon will do if you tell him how I want them—From what of regular rest, I have been rather *narvus*—and the passage in Lear—"Do you not hear the
55 Sea?"—has haunted me intensely. . .

On the Sea

Keats wrote this poem in 1817 when he was staying on the Isle of Wight. It was included in his letter of 17 April to John Hamilton Reynolds that appears on page 9.

4 *Hecate* – a goddess thought to have power over the earth, the heavens and the sea, and therefore in control of the tide.

9 *vexed* – irritated.

14 *quired* – sang as a choir.

> What links are there between the way Keats addresses the reader in this poem and in Ode on Melancholy?

Endymion

The extracts printed are from a substantial poem (four books of approximately 1000 lines per book) written in 1817 and published in 1818. The poem is based on the Greek legend of Endymion, the shepherd who gained immortality through his love of Cynthia, the moon goddess. (See the extract from Keats's letter to Fanny Keats, dated 10 September 1817 (page 23), for a summary of the story.)

232–306 These lines are spoken by a priest who is making a sacrifice to Pan, the rural god, on behalf of the shepherds.

236 *hamadryads* – tree nymphs.

On the Sea

IT keeps eternal whisperings around
   Desolate shores, and with its mighty swell
   Gluts twice ten thousand caverns, till the spell
Of Hecate leaves them their old shadowy sound.
5 Often 'tis in such gentle temper found,
   That scarcely will the very smallest shell
   Be moved for days from where it sometime fell,
When last the winds of heaven were unbound.
Oh ye! who have your eye-balls vexed and tired,
10 Feast them upon the wideness of the Sea;
   Oh ye! whose ears are dinn'd with uproar rude,
Or fed too much with cloying melody,—
   Sit ye near some old cavern's mouth, and brood
Until ye start, as if the sea-nymphs quired!

Extracts from
Endymion

BOOK I. LINES 232–306
 'O THOU, whose mighty palace roof doth hang
From jagged trunks, and overshadoweth
Eternal whispers, glooms, the birth, life, death
235 Of unseen flowers in heavy peacefulness;
Who lov'st to see the hamadryads dress
Their ruffled locks where meeting hazels darken;
And through whole solemn hours dost sit, and hearken

243   *Syrinx* – a nymph who changed into a reed to escape from Pan.

246   *Pan* – the son of Mercury and god of all inhabitants of the countryside.
247   *turtles* – turtle doves.
248   *myrtles* – trees held sacred to Venus, the goddess of love.

252   *foredoom* – dedicate beforehand.
253   *girted* – striped.
254   *leas* – meadows, arable land.

263   *faun and satyr* – minor rural deities, half-man and half-goat.

267   *maw* – stomach (especially of an animal).

272   *Naiads* – water-nymphs.

The dreary melody of bedded reeds—
240 In desolate places, where dank moisture breeds
The pipy hemlock to strange overgrowth;
Bethinking thee, how melancholy loth
Thou wast to lose fair Syrinx—do thou now,
By thy love's milky brow!
245 By all the trembling mazes that she ran,
Hear us, great Pan!

'O thou, for whose soul-soothing quiet, turtles
Passion their voices cooingly 'mong myrtles,
What time thou wanderest at eventide
250 Through sunny meadows, that outskirt the side
Of thine enmossed realms: O thou, to whom
Broad leaved fig trees even now foredoom
Their ripen'd fruitage; yellow girted bees
Their golden honeycombs; our village leas
255 Their fairest blossom'd beans and poppied corn;
The chuckling linnet its five young unborn,
To sing for thee; low creeping strawberries
Their summer coolness; pent up butterflies
Their freckled wings; yea, the fresh budding year
260 All its completions—be quickly near,
By every wind that nods the mountain pine,
O forester divine!

'Thou, to whom every faun and satyr flies
For willing service; whether to surprise
265 The squatted hare while in half sleeping fit;
Or upward ragged precipices flit
To save poor lambkins from the eagle's maw;
Or by mysterious enticement draw
Bewildered shepherds to their path again;
270 Or to tread breathless round the frothy main,
And gather up all fancifullest shells
For thee to tumble into Naiads' cells,
And, being hidden, laugh at their out-peeping;

290   *Dryope* – mother of Pan.

295   *bourne* – boundary, domain.
296   *leaven* – yeast.

305   *Paean* – hymn of thanksgiving, joy and triumph.
306   *Mount Lycean* – a place of worship and sacrifice to Zeus, the Greek
       god.

Or to delight thee with fantastic leaping,
275 The while they pelt each other on the crown
With silvery oak apples, and fir cones brown—
By all the echoes that about thee ring,
Hear us, O satyr king!

'O Hearkener to the loud clapping shears,
280 While ever and anon to his shorn peers
A ram goes bleating: Winder of the horn,
When snouted wild-boars routing tender corn
Anger our huntsmen: Breather round our farms,
To keep off mildews, and all weather harms:
285 Strange ministrant of undescribed sounds,
That come a swooning over hollow grounds,
And wither drearily on barren moors:
Dread opener of the mysterious doors
Leading to universal knowledge—see,
290 Great son of Dryope,
The many that are come to pay their vows
With leaves about their brows!

'Be still the unimaginable lodge
For solitary thinkings; such as dodge
295 Conception to the very bourne of heaven,
Then leave the naked brain: be still the leaven,
That spreading in this dull and clodded earth
Gives it a touch ethereal—a new birth:
Be still a symbol of immensity;
300 A firmament reflected in a sea;
An element filling the space between;
An unknown—but no more: we humbly screen
With uplift hands our foreheads, lowly bending,
And giving out a shout most heaven rending,
305 Conjure thee to receive our humble Paean,
Upon thy Mount Lycean!'

777   *becks* – summons, calls (from *beckon*).

780   *alchemiz'd* – transformed as if by alchemy, the pseudo-science of changing base metals into gold.

784   *impregnates* – fills.

786   *Eolian magic* – the magic of Eolus, god of the winds.

790   *Apollo* – god of music and poetry.
791   *clarions* – trumpets.
791   *bruit* – make sound.
792   *Giant Battle* – struggle between the Titans and the Olympians, as referred to in *Hyperion* (see pages 63–115).
794   *Orpheus* – a mythical figure who played the stringed lyre with great skill.

806   *orbed* – rounded.

808   *genders* – creates.

Wherein lies happiness? In that which becks
Our ready minds to fellowship divine,
A fellowship with essence; till we shine,
780 Full alchemiz'd, and free of space. Behold
The clear religion of heaven! Fold
A rose leaf round thy finger's taperness,
And soothe thy lips: hist, when the airy stress
Of music's kiss impregnates the free winds,
785 And with a sympathetic touch unbinds
Eolian magic from their lucid wombs:
Then old songs waken from enclouded tombs;
Old ditties sigh above their father's grave;
Ghosts of melodious prophesyings rave
790 Round every spot where trod Apollo's foot;
Bronze clarions awake, and faintly bruit,
Where long ago a Giant Battle was;
And, from the turf, a lullaby doth pass
In every place where infant Orpheus slept.
795 Feel we these things?—that moment have we stept
Into a sort of oneness, and our state
Is like a floating spirit's. But there are
Richer entanglements, enthralments far
More self-destroying, leading, by degrees,
800 To the chief intensity: the crown of these
Is made of love and friendship, and sits high
Upon the forehead of humanity.
All its more ponderous and bulky worth
Is friendship, whence there ever issues forth
805 A steady splendour; but at the tip-top,
There hangs by unseen film, an orbed drop
Of light, and that is love: its influence,
Thrown in our eyes, genders a novel sense,
At which we start and fret; till in the end,

814   *pith* – core, centre.

815   *nurtured like a pelican brood* – a reference to the myth that the pelican feeds her young with her own blood.

816   *unsating* – unsatisfying.

817   *van* – front.

819   *winnow* – separate. A term used when harvesting corn; the appearance of *chaff* in the next line continues this image.

823   *elysium* – a place where, according to Greek mythology, souls enjoy complete happiness.

837   *mail* – protective scales.

838   *dower* – inheritance.

839   *runnels* – brooks.

Lines 777–842 can be read as a celebration of love. What evidence would you use to support such a reading?

810 Melting into its radiance, we blend,
Mingle, and so become a part of it,—
Nor with aught else can our souls interknit
So wingedly: when we combine therewith,
Life's self is nourished by its proper pith,

815 And we are nurtured like a pelican brood.
Aye, so delicious is the unsating food,
That men, who might have tower'd in the van
Of all the congregated world, to fan
And winnow from the coming step of time

820 All chaff of custom, wipe away all slime
Left by men-slugs and human serpentry,
Have been content to let occasion die,
Whilst they did sleep in love's elysium.
And, truly, I would rather be struck dumb,

825 Than speak against this ardent listlessness:
For I have ever thought that it might bless
The world with benefits unknowingly;
As does the nightingale, upperched high,
And cloister'd among cool and bunched leaves—

830 She sings but to her love, nor e'er conceives
How tiptoe Night holds back her dark-grey hood.
Just so may love, although 'tis understood
The mere commingling of passionate breath,
Produce more than our searching witnesseth:

835 What I know not: but who, of men, can tell
That flowers would bloom, or that green fruit would swell
To melting pulp, that fish would have bright mail,
The earth its dower of river, wood, and vale,
The meadows runnels, runnels pebble-stones,

840 The seed its harvest, or the lute its tones,
Tones ravishment, or ravishment its sweet,
If human souls did never kiss and greet?

To Fanny Keats, 10 September 1817

Written from Oxford where Keats was staying with Benjamin Bailey. Fanny, Keats's sister, was at the time aged fourteen and at boarding school.

4 *a young Man* – Benjamin Bailey of Magdalen Hall, Oxford.

10 *Many years ago . . .* – this paragraph gives a summary of the Greek legend of Endymion, on which Keats based his poem of that name.

To FANNY KEATS

Wednesday 10 Sept. [1817]

...When I saw you last I told you of my intention of going to Oxford and 'tis now a Week since I disembark'd from his Whip-ship's Coach the Defiance in this place. I am living in Magdalen Hall on a visit to a young Man with whom I have not been long
5 acquainted, but whom I like very much—we lead very industrious lives he in general Studies and I in proceeding at a pretty good rate with a Poem which I hope you will see early in the next year—Perhaps you might like to know what I am writing about—I will tell you—

10 Many Years ago there was a young handsome Shepherd who fed his flocks on a Mountain's Side called Latmus—he was a very contemplative sort of a Person and lived solitry among the trees and Plains little thinking—that such a beautiful Creature as the Moon was growing mad in Love with him—However so it was;
15 and when he was asleep on the Grass, she used to come down from heaven and admire him excessively from a long time; and at last could not refrain from car[r]ying him away in her arms to the top of that high Mountain Latmus while he was a dreaming—but I dare say [you] have read this and all the other beautiful Tales
20 which have come down from the ancient times of that beautiful Greece. If you have not let me know and I will tell you more at large of others quite as delightful—

This Oxford I have no doubt is the finest City in the world—it is full of old Gothic buildings—Spires—towers—Quadrangles—
25 Cloisters Groves &[c.] and is surrounded with more Clear streams than ever I saw together—I take a Walk by the Side of one of them every Evening and thank God, we have not had a drop of rain these many days....

Keats wrote this poem to John Hamilton Reynolds in 1817, while he was staying in Oxford and writing the third book of *Endymion*.

8   *visages* – faces.

9   *tassell trencher* – mortar-board; college cap.

12   *dominat* – (Latin) he is in control.

What details of the poem contribute to its light-hearted tone?

To Benjamin Bailey, 22 November 1817

Keats stayed with Benjamin Bailey in Oxford in September. See letter of 10 September 1817 for further details.

Lines rhymed in a Letter received

(by J.H.R.) from Oxford

I

THE Gothic looks solemn,
The plain Doric column
Supports an old Bishop and Crosier;
The mouldering arch,
5   Shaded o'er by a larch
Stands next door to Wilson the Hosier.

II

Vice—that is, by turns,—
O'er pale visages mourns
The black tassell trencher or common hat;
10   The Chantry boy sings,
The Steeple-bell rings,
And as for the Chancellor—*dominat.*

III

There are plenty of trees,
And plenty of ease,
15   And plenty of fat deer for Parsons;
And when it is venison
Short is the benison,—
Then each on a leg or thigh fastens.

To BENJAMIN BAILEY
[Saturday 22 Nov. 1817]
...I wish you knew all that I think about Genius and the Heart—and yet I think you are thoroughly acquainted with my innermost breast in that respect or you could not have known me even thus

long and still hold me worthy to be your dear friend. In passing
5 however I must say of one thing that has pressed upon me lately
and encreased my Humility and capability of submission and that
is this truth—Men of Genius are great as certain ethereal Chemicals operating on the Mass of neutral intellect—by [*for* but] they
have not any individuality, any determined Character. I would call
10 the top and head of those who have a proper self Men of Power—
But I am running my head into a Subject which I am certain I
could not do justice to under five years s[t]udy and 3 vols octavo—
and moreover long to be talking about the Imagination—so my
dear Bailey do not think of this unpleasant affair if possible—do
15 not—I defy any ha[r]m to come of it—I defy—I'll shall write to
Crips this Week and reque[s]t him to tell me all his goings on from
time to time by Letter wherever I may be—it will all go on well—so
don't because you have suddenly discover'd a Coldness in Haydon suffer yourself to be teased. Do not my dear fellow. O I wish
20 I was as certain of the end of all your troubles as that of your
momentary start about the authenticity of the Imagination. I am
certain of nothing but of the holiness of the Heart's affections and
the truth of Imagination—What the imagination seizes as Beauty
must be truth—whether it existed before or not—for I have the
25 same Idea of all our Passions as of Love they are all in their sublime, creative of essential Beauty—In a Word, you may know my
favorite Speculation by my first Book and the little song I sent in
my last—which is a representation from the fancy of the probable
mode of operating in these Matters—The Imagination may be

---

7 *ethereal Chemicals* – the chemical liquid, ether, will extract substances
from the inert mass over which it is poured.

14 *unpleasant affair* – Haydon's letter about Cripps, a young painter.

19 *Haydon* – Benjamin Haydon (1786–1846), a painter of portraits and
topical scenes.

23–24 *Beauty must be truth* – there are links here with the ideas expressed in
the final lines of *Ode on a Grecian Urn*.

30 *Adam's dream* – *Paradise Lost*, Book VIII, 452–90.

30 compared to Adam's dream—he awoke and found it truth.
I am the more zealous in this affair, because I have never yet been
able to perceive how any thing can be known for truth by conse-
quitive reasoning—and yet it must be—Can it be that even the
greatest Philosopher ever arrived at his goal without putting aside
35 numerous objections—However it may be, O for a Life of Sensations rather than of Thoughts! It is 'a Vision in the form of Youth'
a Shadow of reality to come— and this consideration has further
conv[i]nced me for it has come as auxiliary to another favorite
Speculation of mine, that we shall enjoy ourselves here after by
40 having what we called happiness on Earth repeated in a finer tone
and so repeated—And yet such a fate can only befall those who
delight in sensation rather than hunger as you do after Truth—
Adam's dream will do here and seems to be a conviction that
Imagination and its empyreal reflection is the same as human Life
45 and its spiritual repetition. But as I was saying—the simple imaginative Mind may have its rewards in the repeti[ti]on of its own
silent Working coming continually on the spirit with a fine sud-
denness—to compare great things with small—have you never by
being surprised with an old Melody—in a delicious place—by a
50 delicious voice, fe[l]t over again your very speculations and sur-
mises at the time it first operated on your soul—do you not remember forming to yourself the singer's face more beautiful that [*for*
than] it was possible and yet with the elevation of the Moment you
did not think so—even then you were mounted on the Wings of
55 Imagination so high—that the Prototype must be here after—that
delicious face you will see—What a time! I am continually running
away from the subject—sure this cannot be exactly the case with a
complex Mind—one that is imaginative and at the same time careful of its fruits—who would exist partly on sensation partly on
60 thought—to whom it is necessary that years should bring the
philosophic Mind—such an one I consider your's and therefore it
is necessary to your eternal Happiness that you not only drink of
this old Wine of Heaven, which I shall call the redigestion of our
most ethereal Musings on Earth; but also increase in knowledge
65 and know all things....

Endymion

Here the focus is on a state of mind. The 'den' that Keats mentions in the opening line of this extract is described as a Cave of Quietude in line 548.

530   *bier* – a framework on which a corpse is carried before burial.

531   *death-watch tick* – sound of the death-watch beetle.

536   *Semele* – Semele was consumed with flames when her son, Bacchus, was conceived.

Extract from
Endymion

                       There lies a den,
Beyond the seeming confines of the space
Made for the soul to wander in and trace
515   Its own existence, of remotest glooms.
Dark regions are around it, where the tombs
Of buried griefs the spirit sees, but scarce
One hour doth linger weeping, for the pierce
Of new-born woe it feels more inly smart:
520   And in these regions many a venom'd dart
At random flies; they are the proper home
Of every ill: the man is yet to come
Who hath not journeyed in this native hell.
But few have ever felt how calm and well
525   Sleep may be had in that deep den of all.
There anguish does not sting; nor pleasure pall:
Woe-hurricanes beat ever at the gate,
Yet all is still within and desolate.
Beset with painful gusts, within ye hear
530   No sound so loud as when on curtain'd bier
The death-watch tick is stifled. Enter none
Who strive therefore: on the sudden it is won.
Just when the sufferer begins to burn,
Then it is free to him; and from an urn,
535   Still fed by melting ice, he takes a draught—
Young Semele such richness never quaft
In her maternal longing! Happy gloom!
Dark Paradise! where pale becomes the bloom
Of health by due; where silence dreariest
540   Is most articulate; where hopes infest;

545 *Carian* – Endymion, who was a native of Caria in Asia Minor.

> What details does Keats include in this extract from Book IV to suggest that the Cave of Quietude has positive features?

Stanzas

This poem, written in December 1817, has been associated by some with the Cave of Quietude passage in Book IV of *Endymion*.

4 *felicity* – happiness.

Where those eyes are the brightest far that keep
Their lids shut longest in a dreamless sleep.
O happy spirit-home! O wondrous soul!
Pregnant with such a den to save the whole
545 In thine own depth. Hail, gentle Carian!
For, never since thy griefs and woes began,
Hast thou felt so content: a grievious feud
Hath led thee to this Cave of Quietude.

Stanzas

I

IN a drear-nighted December,
    Too happy, happy tree,
Thy branches ne'er remember
    Their green felicity:
5 The north cannot undo them,
With a sleety whistle through them;
Nor frozen thawings glue them
    From budding at the prime.

II

In a drear-nighted December,
10   Too happy, happy brook,
Thy bubblings ne'er remember
    Apollo's summer look;
But with a sweet forgetting,
They stay their crystal fretting,
15 Never, never petting
    About the frozen time.

21 *The feel of not to feel it* – This line appears in Keats's manuscripts.

In printed appearances of this poem line 21 reads 'To know the change and feel it.' Which version do you find more effective? Why?

To George and Thomas Keats, 21 December 1817

Keats wrote this letter to his brothers after they had left London on 13 December for the cleaner air of Teignmouth, for the sake of Tom's health.

1 *Brown & Dilke* – Charles Brown and Charles Wentworth Dilke, two of Keats's literary friends.

6 *Negative Capability* – this famous phrase has been the subject of much discussion. Keats elaborates these ideas in his letter to Woodhouse, 27 October 1818.

9 *Penetralium* – this word has been cited by Andrew Lang to prove that Keats 'had no classical education'.

III

Ah! would 'twere so with many
　　A gentle girl and boy!
　　But were there ever any
20　　Writh'd not at passed joy?
　　The feel of not to feel it,
　　When there is none to heal it,
　　Nor numbed sense to steal it,
　　　Was never said in rhyme.

To GEORGE AND THOMAS KEATS
[Sunday 21 Dec. 1817]

...Brown & Dilke walked with me & back from the Christmas
pantomime. I had not a dispute but a disquisition with Dilke, on
various subjects; several things dovetailed in my mind, & at once
it struck me, what quality went to form a Man of Achievement
5　especially in Literature & which Shakespeare possessed so enor-
mously—I mean Negative Capability, that is when man is capable
of being in uncertainties, Mysteries, doubts, without any irritable
reaching after fact & reason—Coleridge, for instance, would let go
by a fine isolated verisimilitude caught from the Penetralium of
10　mystery, from being incapable of remaining content with half
knowledge. This pursued through Volumes would perhaps take
us no further than this, that with a great poet the sense of Beauty
overcomes every other consideration, or rather obliterates all consideration....

To Mrs Reynolds's Cat

This sonnet, written in 1818, is a parody of a number of sonnets that Milton addressed to the Parliamentarian leaders of his day.

  1 *Grand Climacteric* – critical stage in life.

  6 *latent* – sheathed, concealed.

13 *lists* – tournaments or jousts, an image from mediaeval chivalry.

14 *glass-bottled wall* – a reference to the practice of placing broken glass on walls to deter intruders.

How would you describe the tone of Keats's sonnet?

On sitting down to read King Lear once again

This sonnet was written in January 1818. In the opening lines Keats dismisses a personification of romance before he settles down to read Shakespeare's *King Lear* once again.

  1 *Romance* – understood by some to be a reference to *Endymion* which Keats was revising at the time of writing this sonnet. He was also planning *Hyperion,* an epic of a very different character.

  2 *Syren* – a bewitching figure.

  7 *burn through* – reading *King Lear* is presented as an ordeal by fire, an image which is extended in the final couplet of this sonnet.

  7 *assay* – try.

  9 *Albion* – an ancient name for Britain, the setting for *King Lear*.

14 *Phoenix* – a mythical Arabian bird which was unique and immortal. Every 500 years it burned itself and rose again from the ashes.

What effect is achieved by the lengthened final line which breaks from the pattern of pentameters established in the rest of this sonnet?

To Mrs. Reynolds's Cat

CAT! who hast past thy Grand Climacteric,
    How many mice and Rats hast in thy days
    Destroy'd?—how many tit bits stolen? Gaze
    With those bright languid segments green and prick
5 Those velvet ears—but pr'ythee do not stick
    Thy latent talons in me—and upraise
    Thy gentle mew—and tell me all thy frays
    Of Fish and Mice, and Rats and tender chick.
    Nay look not down, nor lick thy dainty wrists—
10   For all the weezy Asthma,—and for all
    Thy tail's tip is nicked off—and though the fists
    Of many a Maid have given thee many a maul,
    Still is that fur as soft as when the lists
    In youth thou enter'dst on glass-bottled wall.

On sitting down to read King Lear once again

O GOLDEN tongued Romance, with serene lute!
    Fair plumed Syren, Queen of far-away!
    Leave melodizing on this wintry day,
    Shut up thine olden pages, and be mute:
5 Adieu! for, once again, the fierce dispute
    Betwixt damnation and impassion'd clay
    Must I burn through; once more humbly assay
    The bitter-sweet of this Shakespearian fruit:
    Chief Poet! and ye clouds of Albion,
10   Begetters of our deep eternal theme!
    When through the old oak Forest I am gone,
    Let me not wander in a barren dream,
    But, when I am consumed in the fire
    Give me new Phoenix wings to fly at my desire.

To George and Thomas Keats, 23 January 1818

In this letter Keats outlines details of his activities in London for his brothers, George and Thomas, who were still in Teignmouth.

5   *John Bull The Review . . . Furioso* – nineteenth-century plays.

10   *Nota Bene* – perhaps a reference to a play performed in London, December 1816.

...I left off short in my last, just as I began an account of a private theatrical—Well it was of the lowest order, all greasy & oily, insomuch that if they had lived in olden times, when signs were hung over the doors; the only appropriate one for that oily place would
5 have been—a guttered Candle—They played John Bull The Review. & it was to conclude with Bombastes Furioso—I saw from a Box the 1st Act of John Bull, then I went to Drury & did not return till it was over; when by Wells' interest we got behind the scenes. There was not a yard wide all the way round for actors, scene-
10 shifters & interlopers to move in; for 'Nota Bene' the Green Room was under the stage and there was I threatened over & over again to be turned out by the oily scene-shifters—there did I hear a little painted Trollop own, very candidly, that she had failed in Mary, with a "damned if she'd play a serious part again, as long as she
15 lived", & at the same time she was habited as the Quaker in the Review—there was a quarrel & a fat good-natured looking girl in soldiers Clothes wished she had only been a man for Tom's sake— One fellow began a song, but an unlucky finger-point from the Gallery sent him off like a shot, One chap was dressed to kill for
20 the King in Bombastes, & he stood at the edge of the scene in the very sweat of anxiety to show himself, but Alas the thing was not played, the sweetest morsel of the night moreover was, that the musicians began pegging and fagging away at an overture—never did you see faces more in earnest, three times did they play it over,
25 dropping all kinds of correctness & still did not the curtain draw up—Well then they went into a country-dance then into a region they well knew, into their old boonsome Pothouse, & then to see how pompous o' the sudden they turned; how they looked about & chatted; how they did not care a Damn; was a great treat....

When I have fears

This sonnet, written towards the end of January 1818, shows clearly
Shakespeare's influence on Keats' writing via the rhyme scheme
(abab/cdcd/efef/gg) and subject matter – see, for example, Shakespeare's
sonnet which begins 'When I have seen by time's fell hand defaced'.

2 *glean'd* – literally, picked up every grain.

2 *teeming* – literally overflowing.

3 *charact'ry* – letters; writing.

4 *garners* – barns.

> **What idea is Keats exploring in this sonnet?**

Lines on the Mermaid Tavern

Written in February 1818. The Mermaid Tavern in London was frequented
by Elizabethan and Jacobean playwrights such as Ben Jonson and
Shakespeare.

2 *Elysium* – the legendary home of the blessed dead.

12 *bowse* – drink to excess, booze.

When I have fears

WHEN I have fears that I may cease to be
   Before my pen has glean'd my teeming brain,
Before high-piled books, in charact'ry,
   Hold like rich garners the full-ripen'd grain:
5 When I behold, upon the night's starr'd face,
   Huge cloudy symbols of a high romance,
And think that I may never live to trace
   Their shadows, with the magic hand of chance;
And when I feel, fair creature of an hour!
10   That I shall never look upon thee more,
Never have relish in the faery power
   Of unreflecting love!—then on the shore
Of the wide world I stand alone, and think
Till love and fame to nothingness do sink.

Lines on the Mermaid Tavern

SOULS of Poets dead and gone,
What Elysium have ye known,
Happy field or mossy cavern,
Choicer than the Mermaid Tavern?
5 Have ye tippled drink more fine
Than mine host's Canary wine?
Or are fruits of Paradise
Sweeter than those dainty pies
Of venison? O generous food!
10 Drest as though bold Robin Hood
Would, with his maid Marian,
Sup and bowse from horn and can.

17 *sheepskin* – parchment.

To John Hamilton Reynolds, 19 February 1818

John Hamilton Reynolds was an author, critic and lawyer who befriended Keats in 1816.

9 *the two-and thirty Pallaces* – the thirty-two 'places of delight' of Buddhist doctrine.

14 *an odd angle of the Isle* – *The Tempest*, Act 1, scene 2, 223.
15 *girdle round the earth* – *A Midsummer Night's Dream*, Act 2, scene 1, 175.

I have heard that on a day
Mine host's sign-board flew away,
15 Nobody knew whither, till
An astrologer's old quill
To a sheepskin gave the story,
Said he saw you in your glory,
Underneath a new-old sign
20 Sipping beverage divine,
And pledging with contented smack
The Mermaid in the Zodiac.

Souls of Poets dead and gone,
What Elysium have ye known,
25 Happy field or mossy cavern,
Choicer than the Mermaid Tavern?

To JOHN HAMILTON REYNOLDS
[Thursday 19 Feb. 1818]
My dear Reynolds,

I have an idea that a Man might pass a very pleasant life in this
manner—let him on any certain day read a certain page of full
Poesy or distilled Prose and let him wander with it, and muse upon
5 it, and reflect from it, and bring home to it, and prophesy upon it,
and dream upon it—untill it becomes stale—but when will it do
so? Never—When Man has arrived at a certain ripeness in intellect
any one grand and spiritual passage serves him as a starting post
towards all "the two-and thirty Pallaces". How happy is such a
10 "voyage of conception," what delicious diligent Indolence! A doze
upon a Sofa does not hinder it, and a nap upon Clover engenders
ethereal finger-pointings—the prattle of a child gives it wings, and
the converse of middle age a strength to beat them—a strain of
musick conducts to 'an odd angle of the Isle' and when the leaves
15 whisper it puts a 'girdle round the earth'. Nor will this sparing
touch of noble Books be any irreverance to their Writers—for

perhaps the honours paid by Man to Man are trifles in comparison to the Benefit done by great Works to the 'Spirit and pulse of good' by their mere passive existence. Memory should not be called
20 knowledge—Many have original Minds who do not think it—they are led away by Custom—Now it appears to me that almost any Man may like the Spider spin from his own inwards his own airy Citadel—the points of leaves and twigs on which the Spider begins her work are few and she fills the Air with a beautiful circuiting:
25 man should be content with as few points to tip with the fine Webb of his Soul and wave a tapestry empyrean—full of Symbols for his

26 *empyrean* – sublime, formed of pure light or fire.

What point is Keats making in his comparison of Man with Spider?

To John Taylor, 27 February 1818

John Taylor, working with James Hessey, ran the firm which published Keats's poems.

List the axioms that Keats outlines in this letter. Does he achieve these principles in some or all his poems? List what you consider to be appropriate examples against each axiom, giving reasons for your choice.

spiritual eye, of softness for his spiritual touch, of space for his
wandering, of distinctness for his Luxury—But the Minds of Mortals are so different and bent on such diverse Journeys that it may
30 at first appear impossible for any common taste and fellowship to
exist between two or three under these suppositions—It is however quite the contrary—Minds would leave each other in contrary
directions, traverse each other in Numberless points, and all [for at]
last greet each other at the Journeys end—A old Man and a child
35 would talk together and the old Man be led on his Path, and the
child left thinking—Man should not dispute or assert but whisper
results to his neighbour, and thus by every germ of Spirit sucking
the Sap from mould ethereal every human being might become
great, and Humanity instead of being a wide heath of Furse and
40 Briars with here and there a remote Oak or Pine, would become a
grand democracy of Forest Trees....

To JOHN TAYLOR
[Friday] 27 February 1818
...In Poetry I have a few Axioms, and you will see how far I am from
their Centre. 1st I think Poetry should surprise by a fine excess and
not by Singularity—it should strike the Reader as a wording of his
own highest thoughts, and appear almost a Remembrance—2nd Its
5 touches of Beauty should never be half way ther[e] by making the
reader breathless instead of content: the rise, the progress, the setting of imagery should like the Sun come natural natural too him—
shine over him and set soberly although in magnificence leaving
him in the Luxury of twilight—but it is easier to think what Poetry
10 should be than to write it—and this leads me on to another axiom.
That if Poetry comes not as naturally as the Leaves to a tree it had
better not come at all....

Isabella

This is an extract from a poem written in 1818, based on the story of Isabella's thwarted love that appears in Boccaccio's *Decameron*. According to the story Isabella's brothers, having discovered their sister's love for Lorenzo, murder Lorenzo and bury his body in a forest. Keats uses the Italian ottava rima, a stanza of eight iambic pentameters rhyming abababcc.

107   *swelt* – sweat.

108   *torched* – lit by torches.

113   *Ceylon diver* – the pearl diver who, in diving to great depths, might damage his ears (115).

124   *lazar stairs* – stairs where beggers sit. (A lazar was someone suffering from a disfiguring disease, specifically leprosy.)

Isabella: or The Pot of Basil

XIV

105 With her two brothers this fair lady dwelt,
    Enriched from ancestral merchandize,
And for them many a weary hand did swelt
    In torched mines and noisy factories,
And many once proud-quiver'd loins did melt
110 In blood from stinging whip;—with hollow eyes
    Many all day in dazzling river stood,
    To take the rich-ored driftings of the flood.

XV

For them the Ceylon diver held his breath,
    And went all naked to the hungry shark;
115 For them his ears gush'd blood; for them in death
    The seal on the cold ice with piteous bark
Lay full of darts; for them alone did seethe
    A thousand men in troubles wide and dark:
Half-ignorant they turn'd an easy wheel,
120 That set sharp racks at work, to pinch and peel.

XVI

Why were they proud? Because their marble founts
    Gush'd with more pride than do a wretch's tears?—
Why were they proud? Because fair orange-mounts
    Were of more soft ascent than lazar stairs?—
125 Why were they proud? Because red-lin'd accounts
    Were richer than the songs of Grecian years?—
Why were they proud? again we ask aloud,
Why in the name of Glory were they proud?

140 *Egypt's pest* – Egypt's plague, in this instance the plague of blindness.

145 *Boccaccio* – Giovanni Boccaccio (1313–75), Italian writer and poet and
     author of a collection of stories called the *Decameron* which was one of
     the most influential books of the Middle Ages and was freely borrowed
     from by, among others, Chaucer, Shakespeare, Dryden, Keats and
     Tennyson. Keats acknowledges his debt in lines 145–60.
146 *forgiving boon* – the gift of forgiveness.
147 *myrtles* – trees considered emblems of love.
150 *ghittern* – a stringed instrument, like a guitar.

154 *meet* – appropriate.
155 *assail* – attempt.

XVII

Yet were these Florentines as self-retired
130   In hungry pride and gainful cowardice,
As two close Hebrews in that land inspired,
    Paled in and vineyarded from beggar-spies;
The hawks of ship-mast forests—the untired
    And pannier'd mules for ducats and old lies—
135 Quick cat's-paws on the generous stray-away,—
Great wits in Spanish, Tuscan, and Malay.

How was it these same ledger-men could spy
    Fair Isabella in her downy nest?
How could they find out in Lorenzo's eye
140   A straying from his toil? Hot Egypt's pest
Into their vision covetous and sly!
    How could these money-bags see east and west?—
Yet so they did—and every dealer fair
Must see behind, as doth the hunted hare.

XIX

145 O eloquent and famed Boccaccio!
    Of thee we now should ask forgiving boon,
And of thy spicy myrtles as they blow,
    And of thy roses amorous of the moon,
And of thy lilies, that do paler grow
150   Now they can no more hear thy ghittern's tune,
For venturing syllables that ill beseem
The quiet glooms of such a piteous theme.

Grant thou a pardon here, and then the tale
    Shall move on soberly, as it is meet;
155 There is no other crime, no mad assail
    To make old prose in modern rhyme more sweet:

158 *gone* – dead.

159 *stead* – serve, replace.

163 *unconfines* – reveals.

168 *olive trees* – his estates; this detail indicates a marriage arranged for material gain.

179–80 *bent their footing* – made their way.

184 *while cold is in the skies* – before the heat of day.

But it is done—succeed the verse or fail—
    To honour thee, and thy gone spirit greet;
    To stead thee as a verse in English tongue,
160 An echo of thee in the north-wind sung.

XXI

These brethren having found by many signs
    What love Lorenzo for their sister had,
And how she lov'd him too, each unconfines
    His bitter thoughts to other, well nigh mad
165 That he, the servant of their trade designs,
    Should in their sister's love be blithe and glad,
When 'twas their plan to coax her by degrees
To some high noble and his olive-trees.

XXII

And many a jealous conference had they,
170 And many times they bit their lips alone,
Before they fix'd upon a surest way
    To make the youngster for his crime atone;
And at the last, these men of cruel clay
    Cut Mercy with a sharp knife to the bone;
175 For they resolved in some forest dim
To kill Lorenzo, and there bury him.

XXIII

So on a pleasant morning, as he leant
    Into the sun-rise, o'er the balustrade
Of the garden-terrace, towards him they bent
180 Their footing through the dews; and to him said,
'You seem there in the quiet of content,
    'Lorenzo, and we are most loth to invade
'Calm speculation; but if you are wise,
'Bestride your steed while cold is in the skies.

186 *Apennine* – a range of mountains in Italy.

187 *the hot sun count . . . eglantine* – the sun drying the dew on the sweet-briar is compared to the counting of beads on a rosary.

189 *as he was wont* – as he usually was.

195 *matin-song* – morning song.

200 *lattice* – screen of crossed strips with openings.

209 *murder'd* – Keats is heightening the drama by suggesting the death of Lorenzo before it actually takes place.

210 *Arno* – the river on which Florence stands.

211 *straiten'd* – narrow.

212 *bream* – fish.

185 'To-day we purpose, aye, this hour we mount
  'To spur three leagues towards the Apennine;
  'Come down, we pray thee, ere the hot sun count
    'His dewy rosary on the eglantine.'
  Lorenzo, courteously as he was wont,
190 Bow'd a fair greeting to these serpents' whine;
  And went in haste, to get in readiness,
  With belt, and spur, and bracing huntsman's dress.

  And as he to the court-yard pass'd alone,
    Each third step did he pause, and listen'd oft
195 If he could hear his lady's matin-song,
    Or the light whisper of her footstep soft;
  And as he thus over his passion hung,
    He heard a laugh full musical aloft;
  When, looking up, he saw her features bright
200 Smile through an in-door lattice, all delight.

  'Love, Isabel!' said he, 'I was in pain
    'Lest I should miss to bid thee a good morrow;
  'Ah! what if I should lose thee, when so fain
    'I am to stifle all the heavy sorrow
205 'Of a poor three hours' absence? but we'll gain
    'Out of the amorous dark what day doth borrow.
  'Good bye! I'll soon be back.'—'Good bye!' said she:—
  And as he went she chanted merrily.

  So the two brothers and their murder'd man
210 Rode past fair Florence, to where Arno's stream
  Gurgles through straiten'd banks, and still doth fan
    Itself with dancing bulrush, and the bream

213   *freshets* – small streams of fresh water.

221   *break-covert* – breaking into an ambush.

To John Hamilton Reynolds, 3 May 1818

John Hamilton Reynolds, author, critic and lawyer, was a friend of Keats.

  1   *Wordsworth* – William Wordsworth (1770–1850), contemporary poet and
      important literary figure.

  6   *compare human life to a large Mansion of Many Apartments* – in this famous
      comparison, Keats takes the Christian image of heaven as a house with
      many mansions and creates a secular image of his own development.

Keeps head against the freshets. Sick and wan
　　The brothers' faces in the ford did seem,
215　Lorenzo's flush with love.—They pass'd the water
　　Into a forest quiet for the slaughter.

XXVIII

There was Lorenzo slain and buried in,
　　There in that forest did his great love cease;
　　Ah! when a soul doth thus its freedom win,
220　It aches in loneliness—is ill at peace
　　As the break-covert blood-hounds of such sin:
　　They dipp'd their swords in the water, and did tease
　　Their horses homeward, with convulsed spur,
　　Each richer by his being a murderer.

To JOHN HAMILTON REYNOLDS
Sunday 3 May 1818

...I will return to Wordsworth—whether or no he has an extended
vision or a circumscribed grandeur— whether he is an eagle in his
nest, or on the wing—And to be more explicit and to show you
how tall I stand by the giant, I will put down a simile of human life
5　as far as I now perceive it: that is, to the point to which I say we
both have arrived at—Well—I compare human life to a large Mansion of Many Apartments, two of which I can only describe, the
doors of the rest being as yet shut upon me—The first we step into
we call the infant or thoughtless Chamber, in which we remain as
10　long as we do not think—We remain there a long while, and not-
withstanding the doors of the second Chamber remain wide open,
showing a bright appearance, we care not to hasten to it; but are at
length imperceptibly impelled by the awakening of the thinking
principle—within us—we no sooner get into the second Chamber,
15　which I shall call the Chamber of Maiden-Thought, than we
become intoxicated with the light and the atmosphere, we see

nothing but pleasant wonders, and think of delaying there for ever
in delight: However among the effects this breathing is father of is
that tremendous one of sharpening one's vision into the heart and
20 nature of Man—of convincing one's nerves that the World is full
of Misery and Heartbreak, Pain, Sickness and oppression—
whereby This Chamber of Maiden Thought becomes gradually
darken'd and at the same time on all sides of it many doors are set
open—but all dark—all leading to dark passages—We see not the
25 ballance of good and evil. We are in a Mist—*We* are now in that
state—We feel the "burden of the Mystery," To this Point was
Wordsworth come, as far as I can conceive when he wrote 'Tintern
Abbey' and it seems to me that his Genius is explorative of those
dark Passages. Now if we live, and go on thinking, we too shall
30 explore them—he is a Genius and superior [to] us, in so far as he
can, more than we, make discoveries, and shed a light in them—
Here I must think Wordsworth is deeper than Milton—though I
think it has depended more upon the general and gregarious

43 *Comus* – a masque by John Milton (1608–74), first performed at
    Ludlow in 1634.

44 *time of the dismissal of Cod-pieces* – noted as 1761.

> What points does Keats make about the work of Wordsworth and Milton
> when comparing the two in this letter?

To Thomas Keats, 27 June 1818

This letter was written from Ambleside on a journey north with Charles
Brown. Tom, Keats's brother, was still ill and had been left in London.

advance of intellect, than individual greatness of Mind—From the
35 Paradise Lost and the other Works of Milton, I hope it is not too
presuming, even between ourselves to say, his Philosophy, human
and divine, may be tolerably understood by one not much ad-
vanced in years, In his time englishmen were just emancipated
from a great supersitition—and Men had got hold of certain points
40 and resting places in reasoning which were too newly born to be
doubted, and too much opposed by the Mass of Europe not to be
thought etherial and authentically divine—who could gainsay his
ideas on virtue, vice, and Chastity in Comus, just at the time of the
dismissal of Cod-pieces and a hundred other disgraces? who
45 would not rest satisfied with his hintings at good and evil in the
Paradise Lost, when just free from the inquisition and burrning in
Smithfield? The Reformation produced such immediate and great
benefits, that Protestantism was considered under the immediate
eye of heaven, and its own remaining Dogmas and supersititions,
50 then, as it were, regenerated, constituted those resting places and
seeming sure points of Reasoning—from that I have mentioned,
Milton, whatever he may have thought in the sequel, appears to
have been content with these by his writings—He did not think
into the human heart, as Wordsworth has done—Yet Milton as a
55 Philosop[h]er, had sure as great powers as Wordsworth—What is
then to be inferr'd? O many things—It proves there is really a
grand march of intellect—, It proves that a mighty providence
subdues the mightiest Minds to the service of the time being,
whether it be in human Knowledge or Religion....

To THOMAS KEATS

Saturday 27 June 1818

...We arose this morning at six, because we call it a day of rest,
having to call on Wordsworth who lives only two miles hence—
before breakfast we went to see the Ambleside water fall. The
morning beautiful—the walk easy among the hills. We, I may say,
5 fortunately, missed the direct path, and after wandering a little
found it out by the noise—for, mark you, it is buried in trees, in the
bottom of the valley—the stream itself is interesting throughout

with "mazy error over pendant shades." Milton meant a smooth
river—this is buffetting all the way on a rocky bed ever various—
10 but the waterfall itself, which I came suddenly upon, gave me a
pleasant twinge. First we stood a little below the head about half
way down the first fall, buried deep in trees, and saw it streaming
down two more descents to the depth of near fifty feet—then we
went on a jut of rock nearly level with the second fall-head, where
15 the first fall was above us, and the third below our feet still—at the
same time we saw that the water was divided by a sort of cataract
island on whose other side burst out a glorious stream—then the
thunder and the freshness. At the same time the different falls have
as different characters; the first darting down the slate-rock like an
20 arrow; the second spreading out like a fan—the third dashed into
a mist—and the one on the other side of the rock a sort of mixture
of all these. We afterwards moved away a space, and saw nearly
the whole more mild, streaming silverly through the trees. What
astonishes me more than any thing is the tone, the coloring, the
25 slate, the stone, the moss, the rock-weed; or, if I may so say, the
intellect, the countenance of such places. The space, the magnitude
of mountains and waterfalls are well imagined before one sees
them; but this countenance or intellectual tone must surpass every
imagination and defy any remembrance. I shall learn poetry here
30 and shall henceforth write more than ever, for the abstract en-
deavor of being able to add a mite to that mass of beauty which is
harvested from these grand materials, by the finest spirits, and put
into etherial existence for the relish of one's fellows. I cannot think
with Hazlitt that these scenes make man appear little. I never for-
35 got my stature so completely—I live in the eye; and my imagination, surpassed, is at rest....

8 *mazy error over pendant shades* – *Paradise Lost*, Book IV, 239.
34 *Hazlitt* – Keats had attended lectures given by William Hazlitt
(1778–1830) and had read his literary critical works.

Old Meg

This was written in July 1818 while Keats was travelling with Charles Brown
in Scotland. The woman described in this poem is based on Meg Merrilies, a
character in Walter Scott's *Guy Mannering*.

Old Meg

OLD MEG she was a Gipsey,
   And liv'd upon the Moors;
Her bed it was the brown heath turf,
   And her house was out of doors.

5 Her apples were swart blackberries,
   Her currants, pods o'broom;
Her wine was dew of the wild white rose,
   Her book a churchyard tomb.

Her Brothers were the craggy hills,
10 Her Sisters larchen trees;
Alone with her great family
   She liv'd as she did please.

No breakfast had she many a morn,
   No dinner many a noon,
15 And, 'stead of supper, she would stare
   Full hard against the Moon.

But every morn, of woodbine fresh
   She made her garlanding,
And, every night, the dark glen Yew
20 She wove, and she would sing.

And with her fingers, old and brown,
   She plaited Mats o' Rushes,
And gave them to the Cottagers
   She met among the Bushes.

25 *Margaret Queen* – wife of Henry VI.

26 *Amazon* – a race of female warriors.

28 *chip hat* – hat made of woven wood chippings.

Lines written in the Highlands after a Visit to Burns's Country

This poem was written in the second half of July 1818, when Keats was travelling with Charles Brown in Scotland. The title contains a reference to Robert Burns (1759–96), revered by many as the national poet of Scotland.

2 *patriot battle* – battle to defend Scotland.

3 *Druids* – ancient Celts.

8 *smart* – pain.

22 *Palmer* – pilgrim.

<pre>
25   Old Meg was brave as Margaret Queen
         And tall as Amazon;
      An old red blanket cloak she wore,
         A chip hat had she on.
      God rest her aged bones somewhere!
30   She died full long agone!
</pre>

Lines written in the Highlands after a Visit to Burns's Country

<pre>
      THERE is a charm in footing slow across a silent plain,
      Where patriot battle has been fought, when glory had the gain;
      There is a pleasure on the heath where Druids old have been,
      Where mantles grey have rustled by and swept the nettles green;
5   There is a joy in every spot made known by times of old,
      New to the feet, although each tale a hundred times be told;
      There is a deeper joy than all, more solemn in the heart,   ·
      More parching to the tongue than all, of more divine a smart,
      When weary steps forget themselves upon a pleasant turf,
10   Upon hot sand, or flinty road, or sea-shore iron scurf,
      Toward the castle or the cot, where long ago was born
      One who was great through mortal days, and died of fame unshorn;
      Light heather-bells may tremble then, but they are far away;
      Wood-lark may sing from sandy fern,—the Sun may hear his lay;
15   Runnels may kiss the grass on shelves and shallows clear,
      But their low voices are not heard, though come on travels drear;
      Blood-red the Sun may set behind black mountain peaks;
      Blue tides may sluice and drench their time in caves and weedy creeks;
      Eagles may seem to sleep wing-wide upon the air;
20   Ring-doves may fly convuls'd across to some high-cedar'd lair;
      But the forgotten eye is still fast lidded to the ground,
      As Palmer's, that with weariness, mid-desert shrine hath found.
</pre>

28 *a Bard's low cradle* – Burns's birthplace, at Ayr, which Keats had recently visited.

29 *bourn* – boundary.

44 *diadem* – crown.

45 *fast* – steady.

To Thomas Keats, 26 July 1818

Keats and Charles Brown reached Scotland on their walking tour. (See letter of 27 June 1818 for earlier details of this journey.) They took a boat to Staffa where Keats was very impressed by Fingal's Cave.

At such a time the soul's a child, in childhood is the brain;
Forgotten is the wordly heart—alone, it beats in vain.—
25   Aye, if a madman could have leave to pass a healthful day
To tell his forehead's swoon and faint when first began decay,
He might make tremble many a one whose spirit had gone forth
To find a Bard's low cradle-place about the silent North!
Scanty the hour and few the steps beyond the bourn of care,
30   Beyond the sweet and bitter world,–beyond it unaware!
Scanty the hour and few the steps, because a longer stay
Would bar return, and make a man forget his mortal way:
O horrible! to lose the sight of well-remember'd face,
Of Brother's eyes, of Sister's brow—constant to every place;
35   Filling the air, as on we move, with portraiture intense;
More warm than those heroic tints that pain a painter's sense,
When shapes of old come striding by, and visages of old,
Locks shining black, hair scanty grey, and passions manifold.
No, no, that horror cannot be, for at the cable's length
40   Man feels the gentle anchor pull and gladdens in its strength:—
One hour, half-idiot, he stands by mossy waterfull,
But in the very next he reads his soul's memorial:—
He reads it on the mountain's height, where chance he may sit down
Upon rough marble diadem—that hill's eternal crown.
45   Yet be his anchor e'er so fast, room is there for a prayer
That man may never lose his mind on mountains black and bare;
That he may stray league after league some great birthplace to find
And keep his vision clear from speck, his inward sight unblind.

To THOMAS KEATS
Sunday 26 July 1818

...I am puzzled how to give you an Idea of Staffa. It can only be
represented by a first rate drawing—One may compare the surface
of the Island to a roof—this roof is supported by grand pillars of
basalt standing together as thick as honey combs. The finest thing

5   is Fingal's Cave—it is entirely a hollowing out of Basalt Pillars.
Suppose now the Giants who rebelled against Jove had taken a
whole Mass of black columns and bound them together like
bunches of matches—and then with immense Axes had made a
cavern in the body of these columns—of course the roof and floor
10 must be composed of the broken ends of the Columns—such is
fingal's Cave except that the Sea has done the work of excavations
and is continually dashing there—so that we walk along the sides
of the cave on the pillars which are left as if for convenient Stairs—
the roof is arched somewhat gothic wise and the length of some of
15 the entire side pillars is 50 feet—About the island you might seat
an army of Men each on a pillar—The length of the Cave is 120 feet
and from its extremity the view into the sea through the large Arch
at the entrance—the colour of the colums is a sort of black with a
lurking gloom of purple therein—For solemnity and grandeur it
20 far surpasses the finest Cathedrall—At the extremity of the Cave
there is a small perforation into another cave, at which the waters
meeting and buffetting each other there is sometimes produced a
report as of a cannon heard as far as Iona which must be 12 Miles—
As we approached in the boat there was such a fine swell of the sea
25 that the pillars appeared rising immediately out of the crystal—
But it is impossible to describe it—...

Hyperion

This unfinished poem, written between autumn 1818 and spring 1819,
consists of three books (less than four hundred lines each), the third
obviously incomplete. It is based on the Greek myth of the defeat of the
Titans, the old order of gods, by their children who then established
themselves as the gods on Olympus. Keats focuses on the fate of Hyperion
who was eventually overthrown by Apollo.

  3   *eve's one star* – Venus, the 'evening star'.

  4   *Saturn* – leader of the defeated Titans.

13   *naiad* – river nymph.

18   *nerveless* – incapable of effort.

19   *realmless* – without a kingdom. This adjective has been transferred from
      Saturn himself to his eyes.

Hyperion

A Fragment

DEEP in the shady sadness of a vale
Far sunken from the healthy breath of morn,
Far from the fiery noon, and eve's one star,
Sat gray-hair'd Saturn, quiet as a stone,
5   Still as the silence round about his lair;
Forest on forest hung above his head
Like cloud on cloud. No stir of air was there,
Not so much life as on a summer's day
Robs not one light seed from the feather'd grass,
10 But where the dead leaf fell, there did it rest.
A stream went voiceless by, still deadened more
By reason of his fallen divinity
Spreading a shade: the naiad 'mid her reeds
Press'd her cold finger closer to her lips.

15   Along the margin-sand large foot-marks went,
No further than to where his feet had stray'd,
And slept there since. Upon the sodden ground
His old right hand lay nerveless, listless, dead,
Unsceptred; and his realmless eyes were closed;

23 *one* – Thea, Hyperion's wife and sister of Saturn.

27 *Amazon* – member of a race of female warriors.
28 *pigmy* – dwarf.
29 *Achilles* – leader of the Greeks against the Trojans.
30 *Ixion's wheel* – the wheel to which Ixion was bound as punishment in the underworld.
31 *Memphian sphinx* – a huge statue, part animal, part woman, that stands near Memphis in Egypt.

39 *vanward* – foremost, first.

20 While his bow'd head seem'd list'ning to the Earth,
His ancient mother, for some comfort yet.

It seem'd no force could wake him from his place;
But there came one, who with a kindred hand
Touch'd his wide shoulders, after bending low
25 With reverence, though to one who knew it not.
She was a Goddess of the infant world;
By her in stature the tall Amazon
Had stood a pigmy's height: she would have ta'en
Achilles by the hair and bent his neck;
30 Or with a finger stay'd Ixion's wheel.
Her face was large as that of Memphian sphinx,
Pedestal'd haply in a palace court,
When sages look'd to Egypt for their lore.
But oh! how unlike marble was that face:
35 How beautiful, if sorrow had not made
Sorrow more beautiful than Beauty's self.
There was a listening fear in her regard,
As if calamity had but begun;
As if the vanward clouds of evil days
40 Had spent their malice, and the sullen rear
Was with its stored thunder labouring up.
One hand she press'd upon that aching spot
Where beats the human heart, as if just there,
Though an immortal, she felt cruel pain:
45 The other upon Saturn's bended neck
She laid, and to the level of his ear
Leaning with parted lips, some words she spake
In solemn tenour and deep organ tone:
Some mourning words, which in our feeble tongue
50 Would come in these like accents; O how frail
To that large utterance of the early Gods!
'Saturn, look up!—though wherefore, poor old King?
'I have no comfort for thee, no not one:

59 *hoary* – white-haired.

83 *One moon . . . night* – the new moon had passed through four quarters to become the full moon.

87 *couchant* – lying.

'I cannot say, "O wherefore sleepest thou?"
55 'For heaven is parted from thee, and the earth
    'Knows thee not, thus afflicted, for a God;
    'And ocean too, with all its solemn noise,
    'Has from thy sceptre pass'd; and all the air
    'Is emptied of thine hoary majesty.
60 'Thy thunder, conscious of the new command,
    'Rumbles reluctant o'er our fallen house;
    'And thy sharp lightning in unpractised hands
    'Scorches and burns our once serene domain.
    'O aching time! O moments big as years!
65 'All as ye pass swell out the monstrous truth,
    'And press it so upon our weary griefs
    'That unbelief has not a space to breathe.
    'Saturn, sleep on:–O thoughtless, why did I
    'Thus violate thy slumbrous solitude?
70 'Why should I ope thy melancholy eyes?
    'Saturn, sleep on! while at thy feet I weep.'

    As when, upon a tranced summer-night,
    Those green-rob'd senators of mighty woods,
    Tall oaks, branch-charmed by the earnest stars,
75 Dream, and so dream all night without a stir,
    Save from one gradual solitary gust
    Which comes upon the silence, and dies off,
    As if the ebbing air had but one wave;
    So came these words and went; the while in tears
80 She touch'd her fair large forehead to the ground,
    Just where her fallen hair might be outspread
    A soft and silken mat for Saturn's feet.
    One moon, with alteration slow, had shed
    Her silver seasons four upon the night,
85 And still these two were postured motionless,
    Like natural sculpture in cathedral cavern;
    The frozen God still couchant on the earth,

93   *palsied* – trembling.
94   *horrid* – bristling.
94   *aspen-malady* – shaking like the leaves of the aspen tree.

101   *diadem* – crown.
102   *peers* – appears.
102   *front* – forehead.

117   *eterne* – eternal.
118   *lorn* – deprived.

And the sad Goddess weeping at his feet:
Until at length old Saturn lifted up
90 His faded eyes, and saw his kingdom gone,
And all the gloom and sorrow of the place,
And that fair kneeling Goddess; and then spake,
As with a palsied tongue, and while his beard
Shook horrid with such aspen-malady:
95 'O tender spouse of gold Hyperion,
'Thea, I feel thee ere I see thy face;
'Look up, and let me see our doom in it;
'Look up, and tell me if this feeble shape
'Is Saturn's; tell me, if thou hear'st the voice
100 'Of Saturn; tell me, if this wrinkling brow,
'Naked and bare of its great diadem,
'Peers like the front of Saturn. Who had power
'To make me desolate? whence came the strength?
'How was it nurtur'd to such bursting forth,
105 'While Fate seem'd strangled in my nervous grasp?
'But it is so; and I am smother'd up,
'And buried from all godlike exercise
'Of influence benign on planets pale,
'Of admonitions to the winds and seas,
110 'Of peaceful sway above man's harvesting,
'And all those acts which Deity supreme
'Doth ease its heart of love in.—I am gone
'Away from my own bosom: I have left
'My strong identity, my real self,
115 'Somewhere between the throne, and where I sit
'Here on this spot of earth. Search, Thea, search!
'Open thine eyes eterne, and sphere them round
'Upon all space: space starr'd, and lorn of light;
'Space region'd with life-air; and barren void;
120 'Spaces of fire, and all the yawn of hell.—
'Search, Thea, search! and tell me, if thou seest
'A certain shape or shadow, making way

145   *Chaos* – the state out of which the earth was created.

147   *The rebel three* – Saturn's sons, Jupiter, Neptune and Pluto.

152   *covert* – a concealed place in the woods

'With wings or chariot fierce to repossess
'A heaven he lost erewhile: it must—it must
125 'Be of ripe progress—Saturn must be King.
'Yes, there must be a golden victory;
'There must be Gods thrown down, and trumpets blown
'Of triumph calm, and hymns of festival
'Upon the gold clouds metropolitan,
130 'Voices of soft proclaim, and silver stir
'Of strings in hollow shells; and there shall be
'Beautiful things made new, for the surprise
'Of the sky-children; I will give command:
'Thea! Thea! Thea! where is Saturn?'

135   This passion lifted him upon his feet,
And made his hands to struggle in the air,
His Druid locks to shake and ooze with sweat,
His eyes to fever out, his voice to cease.
He stood, and heard not Thea's sobbing deep;
140 A little time, and then again he snatch'd
Utterance thus.—'But cannot I create?
'Cannot I form? Cannot I fashion forth
'Another world, another universe,
'To overbear and crumble this to nought?
145 'Where is another Chaos? Where?'—That word
Found way unto Olympus, and made quake
The rebel three.—Thea was startled up,
And in her bearing was a sort of hope,
As thus she quick-voic'd spake, yet full of awe.
150   'This cheers our fallen house: come to our friends,
'O Saturn! come away, and give them heart;
'I know the covert, for thence came I hither.'
Thus brief; then with beseeching eyes she went
With backward footing through the shade a space:
155 He follow'd, and she turn'd to lead the way

161 *Titans* – the gods who regarded Saturn as their leader.

166 *orbed fire* – circular fire, the sun.
167 *teeming* – flowing copiously.

181 *Aurorian* – linked to Aurora, goddess of dawn.

Through aged boughs, that yielded like the mist
Which eagles cleave upmounting from their nest.

   Meanwhile in other realms big tears were shed,
More sorrow like to this, and such like woe,
160 Too huge for mortal tongue or pen of scribe:
The Titans fierce, self-hid or prison-bound,
Groan'd for the old allegiance once more,
And listen'd in sharp pain for Saturn's voice.
But one of the whole mammoth-brood still kept
165 His sov'reignty, and rule, and majesty;—
Blazing Hyperion on his orbed fire
Still sat, still snuff'd the incense, teeming up
From Man to the sun's God; yet unsecure:
For as among us mortals omens drear
170 Fright and perplex, so also shuddered he—
Not at dog's howl, or gloom-bird's hated screech,
Or the familiar visiting of one
Upon the first toll of his passing-bell,
Or prophesyings of the midnight lamp;
175 But horrors, portion'd to a giant nerve,
Oft made Hyperion ache. His palace bright
Bastion'd with pyramids of glowing gold,
And touched with shade of bronzed obelisks,
Glar'd a blood-red through all its thousand courts,
180 Arches, and domes, and fiery galleries;
And all its curtains of Aurorian clouds
Flush'd angerly: while sometimes eagle's wings,
Unseen before by Gods or wondering men,
Darken'd the place; and neighing steeds were heard,
185 Not heard before by Gods or wondering men.
Also, when he would taste the spicy wreaths
Of incense, breath'd aloft from sacred hills,
Instead of sweets, his ample palate took
Savour of poisonous brass and metal sick:

195   *colossal* – gigantic.

197   *minions* – favoured followers.

206   *tubes* – trumpets.
207   *Zephyrs* – west winds.

209   *vermeil* – red.

216   *Hours* – gods who presided over the changes in the seasons.

221   *cupola* – dome.

190 And so, when harbour'd in the sleepy west,
    After the full completion of fair day,—
    For rest divine upon exalted couch
    And slumber in the arms of melody,
    He pac'd away the pleasant hours of ease
195 With stride colossal, on from hall to hall;
    While far within each aisle and deep recess,
    His winged minions in close clusters stood,
    Amaz'd and full of fear; like anxious men
    Who on wide plains gather in panting troops,
200 When earthquakes jar their battlements and towers.
    Even now, while Saturn, rous'd from icy trance,
    Went step for step with Thea through the woods,
    Hyperion, leaving twilight in the rear,
    Came slope upon the threshold of the west;
205 Then, as he was wont, his palace-door flew ope
    In smoothest silence, save what solemn tubes,
    Blown by the serious Zephyrs, gave of sweet
    And wandering sounds, slow-breathed melodies;
    And like a rose in vermeil tint and shape,
210 In fragrance soft, and coolness to the eye,
    That inlet to severe magnificence
    Stood full blown, for the God to enter in.

    He enter'd, but he enter'd full of wrath
    His flaming robes stream'd out beyond his heels,
215 And gave a roar, as if of earthly fire,
    That scar'd away the meek ethereal Hours
    And made their dove-wings tremble. On he flared,
    From stately nave to nave, from vault to vault,
    Through bowers of fragrant and enwreathed light,
220 And diamond-paved lustrous long arcades,
    Until he reach'd the great main cupola;
    There standing fierce beneath, he stampt his foot,
    And from the basements deep to the high towers

226 *curb* – restraint.

238 *crystalline* – made of crystal.
238 *fanes* – temples.
239 *lucent* – luminous.

246 *Tellus* – Earth, the first being to spring from Chaos. (See note to line 145.)

249 *infant Thunderer, rebel Jove* – Jove (Jupiter), the youngest son of Saturn, had hurled thunderbolts when dethroning his father.

Jarr'd his own golden region; and before
225 The quavering thunder thereupon had ceas'd,
His voice leapt out, despite of godlike curb,
To this result: 'O dreams of day and night!
'O monstrous forms! O effigies of pain!
'O spectres busy in a cold, cold gloom!
230 'O lank-eared Phantoms of black-weeded Pools!
'Why do I know ye? why have I seen ye? why
'Is my eternal essence thus distraught
'To see and to behold these horrors new?
'Saturn is fallen, am I too to fall?
235 'Am I to leave this haven of my rest,
'This cradle of my glory, this soft clime,
'This calm luxuriance of blissful light,
'These crystalline pavilions, and pure fanes,
'Of all my lucent empire? It is left
240 'Deserted, void, nor any haunt of mine.
'The blaze, the splendor, and the symmetry
'I cannot see—but darkness, death and darkness.
'Even here, into my centre of repose,
'The shady visions come to domineer,
245 'Insult, and blind, and stifle my pomp.—
'Fall!—No, by Tellus and her briny robes!
'Over the fiery frontier of my realms
'I will advance a terrible right arm
'Shall scare that infant Thunderer, rebel Jove,
250 'And bid old Saturn take his throne again.'—
He spake, and ceas'd, the while a heavier threat
Held struggle with his throat but came not forth;
For as in theatres of crowded men
Hubbub increases more they call out 'Hush!'
255 So at Hyperion's words the Phantoms pale
Bestirr'd themselves, thrice horrible and cold;
And from the mirror'd level where he stood
A mist arose, as from a scummy marsh.

269   *The planet orb of fire* – the sun.

274   *colure* – an astrological term for each of two imaginary circles dividing the heavens.

276   *nadir* – the lowest point in the heavens, directly opposite to the zenith (277).

282   *swart* – dark.

284   *argent* – silver.

290   *Fain* – willingly.

At this, through all his bulk an agony

260 Crept gradual, from the feet unto the crown,
Like a lithe serpent vast and muscular
Making slow way, with head and neck convuls'd
From over-strained might. Releas'd, he fled
To the eastern gates, and full six dewy hours

265 Before the dawn in season due should blush,
He breath'd fierce breath against the sleepy portals,
Clear'd them of heavy vapours, burst them wide
Suddenly on the ocean's chilly streams.
The planet orb of fire, whereon he rode

270 Each day from east to west the heavens through,
Spun round in sable curtaining of clouds;
Not therefore veiled quite, blindfold, and hid,
But ever and anon the glancing spheres,
Circles, and arcs, and broad-belting colure,

275 Glow'd through, and wrought upon the muffling dark
Sweet-shaped lightnings from the nadir deep
Up to the zenith,—hieroglyphics old,
Which sages and keen-eyed astrologers
Then living on the earth, with labouring thought

280 Won from the gaze of many centuries:
Now lost, save what we find on remnants huge
Of stone, or marble swart; their import gone,
Their wisdom long since fled.—Two wings this orb
Possess'd for glory, two fair argent wings,

285 Ever exalted at the God's approach
And now, from forth the gloom their plumes immense
Rose, one by one, till all outspreaded were;
While still the dazzling globe maintain'd eclipse,
Awaiting for Hyperion's command.

290 Fain would he have commanded, fain took throne
And bid the day begin, if but for change.
He might not:—No, though a primeval God:
The sacred seasons might not be disturb'd.

298 *demesnes* – domains territories.

299 *bright Titan* – Hyperion.

307 *Coelus* – Hyperion's father who had been overthrown by his son.

323 *first-born* – Saturn.

Therefore the operations of the dawn
295 Stay'd in their birth, even as here 'tis told.
Those silver wings expanded sisterly,
Eager to sail their orb; the porches wide
Open'd upon the dusk demesnes of night
And the bright Titan, phrenzied with new woes,
300 Unus'd to bend, by hard compulsion bent
His spirit to the sorrow of the time;
And all along a dismal rack of clouds,
Upon the boundaries of day and night,
He stretch'd himself in grief and radiance faint.
305 There as he lay, the Heaven with its stars
Look'd down on him with pity, and the voice
Of Coelus, from the universal space,
Thus whisper'd low and solemn in his ear.
'O brightest of my children dear, earth-born
310 'And sky-engendered, Son of Mysteries
'All unrevealed even to the powers
'Which met at thy creating; at whose joys
'And palpitations sweet, and pleasures soft,
'I, Coelus, wonder, how they came and whence;
315 'And at the fruits thereof what shapes they be,
'Distinct and visible; symbols divine,
'Manifestations of that beauteous life
'Diffus'd unseen throughout eternal space:
'Of these new-form'd art thou, oh brightest child!
320 'Of these, thy brethren and the Goddesses!
'There is sad feud among ye, and rebellion
'Of son against his sire. I saw him fall,
'I saw my first-born tumbled from his throne!
'To me his arms were spread, to me his voice
325 'Found way from forth the thunders round his head!
'Pale was I, and in vapours hid my face.
'Art thou, too, near such doom? vague fear there is:
'For I have seen my sons most unlike Gods.

Book II

4   *Cybele* – wife of Saturn.

'Divine ye were created, and divine
330 'In sad demeanour, solemn, undisturb'd,
'Unruffled, like high Gods, ye liv'd and ruled:
'Now I behold in you fear, hope, and wrath;
'Actions of rage and passion; even as
'I see them, on the mortal world beneath,
335 'In men who die.—This is the grief, O Son!
'Sad sign of ruin, sudden dismay, and fall!
'Yet do thou strive; as thou art capable,
'As thou canst move about, an evident God;
'And canst oppose to each malignant hour
340 'Ethereal presence:—I am but a voice;
'My life is but the life of winds and tides,
'No more than winds and tides can I avail:—
'But thou canst.—Be thou therefore in the van
'Of Circumstance; yea, seize the arrow's barb
345 'Before the tense string murmur.—To the earth!
'For there thou wilt find Saturn, and his woes.
'Meantime I will keep watch on thy bright sun,
'And of thy seasons be a careful nurse.'—
Ere half this region-whisper had come down,
350 Hyperion arose, and on the stars
Lifted his curved lids, and kept them wide
Until it ceas'd; and still he kept them wide:
And still they were the same bright, patient stars
Then with a slow incline of his broad breast,
355 Like to a diver in the pearly seas,
Forward he stoop'd over the airy shore,
And plung'd all noiseless into the deep night.

BOOK II

JUST at the self-same beat of Time's wide wings
Hyperion slid into the rustled air,
And Saturn gain'd with Thea that sad place
Where Cybele and the bruised Titans mourn'd.

19 *Coeus . . . Porphyrion* – all gods and Titans, except Dolor who is
    considered to be Keats's personification of grief.

28 *sanguine* – of the blood.
29 *Mnemosyne* – Memory.
30 *Phoebe* – Phoebe, the Titan, was grandmother to Phoebe, the moon
    goddess.

34 *cirque* – circle.

39 *kept shroud* – was hidden in darkness.

5   It was a den where no insulting light
     Could glimmer on their tears; where their own groans
     They felt, but heard not, for the solid roar
     Of thunderous waterfalls and torrents hoarse,
     Pouring a constant bulk, uncertain where.
10 Crag jutting forth to crag, and rocks that seem'd
     Ever as if just rising from a sleep,
     Forehead to forehead held their monstrous horns;
     And thus in thousand hugest phantasies
     Made a fit roofing to this nest of woe.
15 Instead of thrones, hard flint they sat upon,
     Couches of rugged stone, and slaty ridge
     Stubborn'd with iron. All were not assembled:
     Some chain'd in torture, and some wandering.
     Coeus, and Gyges, and Briareüs,
20 Typhon, and Dolor, and Porphyrion,
     With many more, the brawniest in assault,
     Were pent in regions of laborious breath;
     Dungeon'd in opaque element, to keep
     Their clenched teeth still clench'd, and all their limbs
25 Lock'd up like veins of metal, crampt and screw'd;
     Without a motion, save of their big hearts
     Heaving in pain, and horribly convuls'd
     With sanguine feverous boiling gurge of pulse.
     Mnemosyne was straying in the world;
30 Far from her moon had Phoebe wandered;
     And many else were free to roam abroad,
     But for the main, here found they covert drear.
     Scarce images of life, one here, one there,
     Lay vast and edgeways; like a dismal cirque
35 Of Druid stones, upon a forlorn moor,
     When the chill rain begins at shut of eve,
     In dull November, and their chancel vault,
     The Heaven itself, is blinded throughout night.
     Each one kept shroud, nor to his neighbour gave

41   *Creüs* – brother of Saturn.

44   *Iapetüs* – brother of Saturn.

46   *gorge* – throat.

49   *Cottus* – brother of Saturn.

53   *Asia* – Keats describes this god as daughter of Caf, a mythical mountain in
     Persia, and Tellus. (See note to Book I, line 246.)

60   *Oxus* – river in Asia.

66   *Enceladus* – a Titan renowned for his strength.

73   *Atlas* – a Titan who was later condemned to bear the heavens on his
     shoulders.
74   *Phorcus* – a sea god.
74   *Gorgons* – three hideous sisters with serpent hair, whose glance turned
     mortals to stone. Two were immortal but the third, Medusa, was killed
     by Perseus who cut off her head and gave it to Athene the goddess of
     wisdom.

40 Or word, or look, or action of despair.
   Creüs was one; his ponderous iron mace
   Lay by him, and a shatter'd rib of rock
   Told of his rage, ere he thus sank and pined.
   Iapetüs another; in his grasp,
45 A serpent's plashy neck; its barbed tongue
   Squeez'd from the gorge, and all its uncurl'd length
   Dead; and because the creature could not spit
   Its poison in the eyes of conquering Jove.
   Next Cottus: prone he lay, chin uppermost,
50 As though in pain; for still upon the flint
   He ground severe his skull, with open mouth
   And eyes at horrid working. Nearest him
   Asia, born of most enormous Caf,
   Who cost her mother Tellus keener pangs
55 Though feminine, than any of her sons:
   More thought than woe was in her dusky face,
   For she was prophesying of her glory;
   And in her wide imagination stood
   Palm-shaded temples, and high rival fanes,
60 By Oxus or in Ganges' sacred isles.
   Even as Hope upon her anchor leans,
   So leant she, not so fair, upon a tusk
   Shed from the broadest of her elephants.
   Above her, on a crag's uneasy shelve,
65 Upon his elbow rais'd, all prostrate else,
   Shadow'd Enceladus; once tame and mild
   As grazing ox unworried in the meads;
   Now tiger-passion'd, lion-thoughted, wroth,
   He meditated, plotted, and even now
70 Was hurling mountains in that second war,
   Not long delay'd, that scar'd the younger Gods
   To hide themselves in forms of beast and bird.
   Not far hence Atlas; and beside him prone
   Phorcus, the sire of Gorgons. Neighbour'd close

75 *Oceanus* – god of the waters and married to Tethys.

76 *Clymene* – daughter of Oceanus and Tethys.

77 *Themis* – one of the Titans.

78 *Ops* – another name for Cybele, Saturn's wife.

95 *spleen* – anger.

97 *mortal oil . . . disanointing poison* – an oil depriving him of his position as king of the gods.

99 *her still* – herself still.

107 *Enceladus* – see note line 66 above.

75 Oceanus, and Tethys, in whose lap
   Sobb'd Clymene among her tangled hair.
   In midst of all lay Themis, at the feet
   Of Ops the queen; all clouded round from sight,
   No shape distinguishable, more than when
80 Thick night confounds the pine-tops with the clouds:
   And many else whose names may not be told.
   For when the Muse's wings are air-ward spread,
   Who shall delay her flight? And she must chaunt
   Of Saturn, and his guide, who now had climb'd
85 With damp and slippery footing from a depth
   More horrid still. Above a sombre cliff
   Their heads appear'd, and up their stature grew
   Till on the level height their steps found ease:
   Then Thea spread abroad her trembling arms
90 Upon the precincts of this nest of pain,
   And sidelong fix'd her eye on Saturn's face:
   There saw she direst strife; the supreme God
   At war with all the frailty of grief,
   Of rage, of fear, anxiety, revenge,
95 Remorse, spleen, hope, but most of all despair.
   Against these plagues he strove in vain; for Fate
   Had pour'd a mortal oil upon his head
   A disanointing poison: so that Thea,
   Affrighted, kept her still, and let him pass
100 First onwards in, among the fallen tribe.

    As with us mortal men, the laden heart
    Is persecuted more, and fever'd more,
    When it is nighing to the mournful house
    Where other hearts are sick of the same bruise;
105 So Saturn, as he walke'd into the midst,
    Felt faint, and would have sunk among the rest,
    But that he met Enceladus's eye,
    Whose mightiness, and awe of him, at once

134   *Uranus* – god of the skies, father of Saturn.

Came like an inspiration; and he shouted,
110 'Titans, behold your God!' at which some groan'd;
Some started on their feet; some also shouted;
Some wept, some wail'd, all bow'd with reverence;
And Ops, uplifting her black folded veil,
Show'd her pale cheeks, and all her forehead wan,
115 Her eye-brows thin and jet, and hollow eyes.
There is a roaring in the bleak-grown pines
When Winter lifts his voice; there is a noise
Among immortals when a God gives sign,
With hushing finger, how he means to load
120 His tongue with the full weight of utterless thought,
With thunder, and with music, and with pomp:
Such noise is like the roar of bleak-grown pines;
Which, when it ceases in this mountain'd world,
No other sound succeeds; but ceasing here,
125 Among these fallen, Saturn's voice therefrom
Grew up like organ, that begins anew
Its strain, when other harmonies, stopt short,
Leave the dinn'd air vibrating silverly.
Thus grew it up—'Not in my own sad breast,
130 'Which is its own great judge and searcher out,
'Can I find reasons why ye should be thus:
'Not in the legend of the first of days,
'Studied from that old spirit-leaved book
'Which starry Uranus with finger bright
135 'Sav'd from the shores of darkness, when the waves
'Low-ebb'd still hid it up in shallow gloom;—
'And the which book ye know I ever kept
'For my firm-based footstool: Ah, infirm!
'Not there, nor in sign, symbol, or portent
140 'Of element, earth, water, air, and fire,—
'At war, at peace, or inter-quarrelling
'One against one, or two, or three, or all
'Each several one against the other three,

161   *engine* – move into action.

165   *astonied* – astonished.

167   *God of the Sea* – Uranus.
168   *Sophist and sage* – philosopher and wise man.

176   *ire* – anger.

'As fire with air loud warring when rain-floods
145 'Drown both, and press them both against earth's face.
'Where, finding sulphur, a quadruple wrath
'Unhinges the poor world;—not in that strife,
'Wherefrom I take strange lore, and read it deep,
'Can I find reason why ye should be thus:
150 'No, no-where can unriddle, though I search,
'And pore on Nature's universal scroll
'Even to swooning, why ye, Divinities,
'The first-born of all shap'd and palpable Gods.
'Should cower beneath what, in comparison,
155 'Is untremendous might. Yet ye are here,
'O'erwhelmed, and spurn'd, and batter'd, ye are here!
'O Titans, shall I say "Arise!"—ye groan:
'Shall I say "Crouch!"—Ye groan. What can I then?
'O Heaven wide! O unseen parent dear!
160 'What can I? Tell me, all ye brethren Gods,
'How we can war, how engine our great wrath!
'O speak your counsel now, for Saturn's ear
'Is all a-hunger'd. Thou, Oceanus,
'Ponderest high and deep; and in thy face
165 'I see, astonied, that severe content
'Which comes of thought and musing: give us help!'

    So ended Saturn; and the God of the Sea,
Sophist and sage, from no Athenian grove,
But cogitation in his watery shades,
170 Arose, with locks not oozy, and began,
In murmurs, which his first-endeavouring tongue
Caught infant-like from the far-foamed sands.
'O ye, whom wrath consumes! who, passion-stung,
'Writhe at defeat, and nurse your agonies!
175 'Shut up your senses, stifle up your ears,
'My voice is not a bellows unto ire.
'Yet listen, ye who will, whilst I bring proof

191   *Chaos* – the bottomless abyss which, according to Greek myth, was the first of all existing things. From it was born Gaea, the mother and wife of Uranus.

'How ye, perforce, must be content to stoop:
'And in the proof much comfort will I give,
180 'If ye will take that comfort in its truth.
'We fall by course of Nature's law, not force
'Of thunder, or of Jove. Great Saturn, thou
'Hast sifted well the atom-universe;
'But for this reason, that thou art the King,
185 'And only blind from sheer supremacy,
'One avenue was shaded from thine eyes,
'Through which I wandered to eternal truth.
'And first, as thou wast not the first of powers,
'So art thou not the last; it cannot be:
190 'Thou art not the beginning nor the end.
'From Chaos and parental Darkness came
'Light, the first fruits of that intestine broil,
'That sullen ferment, which for wondrous ends
'Was ripening in itself. The ripe hour came,
195 'And with it Light, and Light, engendering
'Upon its own producer, forthwith touched,
'The whole enormous matter into Life,
'Upon that very hour, our parentage,
'The Heavens and the Earth, were manifest:
200 'Then thou first born, and we the giant race,
'Found ourselves ruling new and beauteous realms.
'Now comes the pain of truth, to whom 'tis pain;
'O folly! for to bear all naked truths,
'And to envisage circumstance, all calm,
205 'That is the top of sovereignty. Mark well!
'As Heaven and Earth are fairer, fairer far
'Than Chaos and blank Darkness, though once chiefs;
'As as we show beyond that Heaven and Earth
'In form and shape compact and beautiful,
210 'In will, in action free, companionship,
'And thousand other signs of purer life;
'Soon on our heels a fresh perfection treads,

·

232   *young God of the Seas* – Neptune.

'A power more strong in beauty, born of us
'And fated to excel us, as we pass
215 'In glory that old Darkness: nor are we
'Thereby more conquer'd, than by us the rule
'Of shapeless Chaos. Say, doth the dull soil
'Quarrel with the proud forests it hath fed,
'And feedeth still, more comely than itself?
220 'Can it deny the chiefdom of green groves?
'Or shall the tree be envious of the dove
'Because it cooeth, and hath snowy wings
'To wander wherewithal, and find its joys?
'We are such forest-trees, and our fair boughs
225 'Have bred forth, not pale solitary doves,
'But eagles golden-feather'd, who do tower
'Above us in their beauty, and must reign
'In right thereof; for 'tis the eternal law
'That first in beauty should be first in might:
230 'Yea, by that law, another race may drive
'Our conquerors to mourn as we do now.
'Have ye beheld the young God of the Seas,
'My dispossessor? Have ye seen his face?
'Have ye beheld his chariot, foam'd along
235 'By noble winged creatures he hath made?
'I saw him on the calmed waters scud,
'With such a glow of beauty in his eyes
'That it enforced me to bid sad farewell
'To all my empire: farewell sad I took,
240 'And hither came, to see how dolorous fate
'Had wrought upon ye; and how I might best
'Give consolation in this woe extreme.
'Receive the truth, and let it be your balm.'

Whether through poz'd conviction, or disdain,
245 They guarded silence, when Oceanus
Left murmuring, what deepest thought can tell?

248   *Clymene* – see note to Book II, line 76.

250   *hectic* – flushed, agitated.

But so it was, none answer'd for a space,
Save one whom none regarded, Clymene;
And yet she answer'd not, only complain'd,
250 With hectic lips, and eyes up-looking mild,
Thus wording timidly among the fierce:
'O Father, I am here the simplest voice,
'And all my knowledge is that joy is gone,
'And this thing woe crept in among our hearts,
255 'There to remain for ever, as I fear:
'I would not bode of evil, if I thought
'So weak a creature could turn off the help
'Which by just right should come of mighty Gods;
'Yet let me tell my sorrow, let me tell
260 'Of what I heard, and how it made me weep,
'And know that we had parted from all hope.
'I stood upon a shore, a pleasant shore,
'Where a sweet clime was breathed from a land
'Of fragrance, quietness, and trees, and flowers.
265 'Full of calm joy it was, as I of Grief;
'Too full of joy and soft delicious warmth;
So that I felt a movement in my heart
'To chide, and to reproach that solitude
'With songs of misery, music of our woes;
270 'And sat me down, and took a mouthed shell
'And murmur'd into it, and made melody—
'O melody no more! for while I sang,
'And with poor skill let pass into the breeze
'The dull shell's echo, from a bowery strand
275 'Just opposite, an island of the sea,
'There came enchantment with the shifting wind,
'That did both drown and keep alive my ears.
'I threw my shell away upon the sand,
'And a wave filled it, as my sense was fill'd
280 'With that new blissful golden melody.
'A living death was in each gush of sounds,

286 *dove . . . olive* – both symbols of peace.

'Each family of rapturous hurried notes,
'That fell, one after one, yet all at once,
'Like pearl beads dropping sudden from their string:
285 'And then another, then another strain,
'Each like a dove leaving its olive perch,
'With music win'd instead of silent plumes,
'To hover round my head, and make me sick
'Of joy and grief at once. Grief overcame,
290 'And I was stopping up my frantic ears,
'When, past all hindrance of my trembling hands,
'A voice came sweeter, sweeter than all tune,
'And still it cried, "Apollo! young Apollo!"
'"The morning-bright Apollo! Young Apollo!"
295 'I fled, it follow'd me, and cried "Apollo!"
'O Father, and O Brethren, had ye felt
'Those pains of mine; O Saturn, hadst thou felt,
'Ye would not call this too indulged tongue
'Presumptuous, in thus venturing to be heard.'

300 So far her voice flow'd on, like timorous brook
That, lingering along a pebbled coast,
Doth fear to meet the sea: but sea it met,
And shudder'd; for the overwhelming voice
Of huge Enceladus swallow'd it in wrath:
305 The ponderous syllables, like sullen waves
In the half-glutted hollows of reef-rocks,
Came booming thus, while still upon his arm
He lean'd; not rising, from supreme contempt.
'Or shall we listen to the over-wise,
310 'Or to the over-foolish, Giant-Gods?
'Not thunderbolt on thunderbolt, till all
'That rebel Jove's whole armoury were spent,
'Not world on world upon these shoulders piled,
'Could agonize me more than baby-words
315 'In midst of this dethronement horrible.

341 *winged thing* – In classical sculpture, Nike, the goddess of victory, was traditionally represented with wings.

'Speak! roar! shout! yell! ye sleepy Titans all.
'Do ye forget the blows, the buffets vile?
'Are ye not smitten by a youngling arm?
'Dost thou forget, sham Monarch of the Waves,
320 'Thy scalding in the seas? What, have I rous'd
'Your spleens with so few simple words as these?
O joy! for now I see ye are not lost:
'O joy! for now I see a thousand eyes
'Wide-glaring for revenge!'—As this he said,
325 He lifted up his stature vast and stood,
Still without intermission speaking thus:
'Now ye are flames, I'll tell you how to burn,
'And purge the ether of our enemies;
'How to feed fierce the crooked stings of fire,
330 'And singe away the swollen clouds of Jove,
'Stifling that puny essence in its tent.
'O let him feel the evil he hath done;
'For though I scorn Oceanus's lore,
'Much pain have I for more than loss of realms:
335 'The days of peace and slumberous calm are fled;
'Those days all innocent of scathing war,
'When all the fair Existences of heaven
'Came open-eyed to guess what we would speak:—
'That was before our brows were taught to frown,
340 'Before our lips knew else but solemn sounds;
'That was before we knew the winged thing,
'Victory might be lost, or might be won.
'And be ye mindful that Hyperion,
'Our brightest brother, still is undisgraced—
345 'Hyperion, lo! his radiance is here!'

All eyes were on Enceladus's face,
And they beheld, while still Hyperion's name
Flew from his lips up to the vaulted rocks,
A pallid gleam across his features stern:
350 Not savage, for he saw full many a God

371 *Numidian curl* – a reference to the curly hair of the Numidian peoples who lived on the north coast of Africa (roughly present-day Algeria).

374 *Memnon* – son of Aurora, goddess of dawn. In later antiquity, he became associated with the colossal statue of Amenophis near Thebes in Egypt, known as the 'column of Memnon'.

376 *Memnon's harp* – after its partial destruction by an earthquake in 27BC, the statue was said to emit a musical sound when touched by the first rays of the rising sun.

Wroth as himself. He look'd upon them all,
And in each face he saw a gleam of light,
But splendider in Saturn's, whose hoar locks
Shone like the bubbling foam about a keel
355 When the prow sweeps into a midnight cove.
In pale and silver silence they remain'd,
Till suddenly a splendour, like the morn,
Pervaded all the beetling gloomy steeps,
All the sad spaces of oblivion,
360 And every gulf, and every chasm old,
And every height, and every sullen depth,
Voiceless, or hoarse with loud tormented streams:
And all the everlasting cataracts,
And all the headlong torrents far and near,
365 Mantled before in darkness and huge shade,
Now saw the light and made it terrible.
It was Hyperion:—a granite peak
His bright feet touch'd, and there he stay'd to view
The misery his brilliance had betray'd
370 To the most hateful seeing of itself.
Golden his hair of short Numidian curl,
Regal his shape majestic, a vast shade
In midst of his own brightness, like the bulk
Of Memnon's image at the set of sun
375 To one who travels from the dusking East:
Sighs, too, as mournful as that Memnon's harp
He utter'd, while his hands contemplative
He press'd together, and in silence stood.
Despondence seiz'd again the fallen Gods
380 At sight of the dejected King of Day,
And many hid their faces from the light:
But fierce Enceladus sent forth his eyes
Among the brotherhood; and, at their glare,
Uprose Iäpetus, and Creüs too,
385 And Phorcus, sea-born, and together strode

389 *Mother of the Gods* – Ops, Saturn's wife.

Book III

  2 *Amazed* – distracted.
  3 *Muse* – the Muses were the nine daughters of Jupiter and Mnemosyne. They represented the various types of poetry, arts and sciences. The reference here is to Melpomene, the Muse of tragedy.

 10 *Delphic harp* – the lyre of Apollo, who was the god of music and poetry and whose principle shrine was at Delphi.
 12 *Dorian* – a style of music which is both simple and solemn.
 13 *Father of all verse* – Apollo.
 14 *vermeil* – red.

 23 *Cyclades* – a group of islands in the Aegean Sea which lay in a circle around Delos (24), the birthplace of Apollo.

To where he towered on his eminence.
There those four shouted forth old Saturn's name;
Hyperion from the peak loud answered, 'Saturn!'
Saturn sat near the Mother of the Gods,
390 In whose face was no joy, though all the Gods
Gave from their hollow throats the name of 'Saturn!'

BOOK III
THUS in alternate uproar and sad peace,
Amazed were those Titans utterly.
O leave them, Muse! O leave them to their woes;
For thou art weak to sing such tumults dire:
5   A solitary sorrow best befits
Thy lips, and antheming a lonely grief.
Leave them, O Muse! for thou anon wilt find
Many a fallen old Divinity
Wandering in vain about bewildered shores.
10   Meantime touch piously the Delphic harp,
And not a wind of heaven but will breathe
In aid soft warble from the Dorian flute;
For lo! 'tis for the Father of all verse.
Flush every thing that hath a vermeil hue,
15   Let the rose glow intense and warm the air,
And let the clouds of even and of morn
Float in voluptuous fleeces o'er the hills;
Let the red wine within the goblet boil,
Cold as a bubbling well; let faint-lipp'd shells,
20   On sands, or in great deeps, vermilion turn
Through all their labyrinths; and let the maid
Blush keenly, as with some warm kiss surpris'd.
Chief isle of the embowered Cyclades,
Rejoice, O Delos, with thine olives green,
25   And poplars, and lawn-shading palms, and beech,

26   *Zephyr* – see note to Book I, line 207.

29   *Giant of the Sun* – Hyperion.

31   *his mother* – Latona, the daughter of Zeus and Phoebe.
32   *twin-sister* – Diana.

34   *osiers* – willows.

46   *an awful Goddess* – Mnemosyne, goddess of memory.

51   *mien* – presence, bearing.

In which the Zephyr breathes the loudest song,
And hazels thick, dark-stemm'd beneath the shade:
Apollo is once more the golden theme!
Where was he, when the Giant of the Sun
30 Stood bright, amid the sorrow of his peers?
Together had he left his mother fair
And his twin-sister sleeping in their bower,
And in the morning twilight wandered forth
Beside the osiers of a rivulet,
35 Full ankle-deep in lilies of the vale.
The nightingale had ceas'd, and a few stars
Were lingering in the heavens, while the thrush
Began calm-throated. Throughout all the isle
There was no covert, no retired cave
40 Unhaunted by the murmurous noise of waves,
Though scarcely heard in many a green recess.
He listen'd, and he wept, and his bright tears
Went trickling down the golden bow he held.
Thus with half-shut suffused eyes he stood,
45 While from beneath some cumbrous boughs hard by
With solemn step an awful Goddess came,
And there was purport in her looks for him,
Which he with eager guess began to read
Perplex'd, the while melodiously he said:
50 'How cam'st thou over the unfooted sea?
'Or hath that antique mien and robed form
'Mov'd in these vales invisible till now?
'Sure I have heard those vestments sweeping o'er
'The fallen leaves, when I have traced
55 'In cool mid-forest. Surely I have traced
'The rustle of those ample skirts about
'These grassy solitudes, and seen the flowers
'Lift up their heads, as still the whisper pass'd.
'Goddess! I have beheld those eyes before,
60 'And their eternal calm, and all that face,

63 *lyre* – stringed musical instrument, like a harp.

92 *liegeless* – without master.
93 *aspirant* – aspiring, ascending.

'Or I have dream'd.'—'Yes,' said the supreme shape,
'Thou hast dream'd of me; and awaking up
'Didst find a lyre all golden by thy side,
'Whose strings touch'd by thy fingers, all the vast
65 'Unwearied ear of the whole universe
'Listen'd in pain and pleasure at the birth
'Of such new tuneful wonder. Is't not strange
'That thou shouldst weep, so gifted? Tell me, youth,
'What sorrow thou canst feel; for I am sad
70 'When thou dost shed a tear: explain thy griefs
'To one who in this lonely isle hath been
'The watcher of thy sleep and hours of life,
'From the young day when first thy infant hand
'Pluck'd witless the weak flowers, till thine arm
75 'Could bend that bow heroic to all times.
'Show thy heart's secret to an ancient Power
'Who hath forsaken old and sacred thrones
'For prophecies of thee, and for the sake
'Of loveliness new born.'—Apollo then,
80 With sudden scrutiny and gloomless eyes,
Thus answer'd, while his white melodious throat
Throbb'd with the syllables.—'Mnemosyne!
'Thy name is on my tongue, I know not how;
'Why should I tell thee what thou so well seest?
85 'Why should I strive to show what from thy lips
'Would come to no mystery? For me, dark, dark,
'And painful vile oblivion seals my eyes:
'I strive to search wherefore I am so sad,
'Until a melancholy numbs my limbs:
90 'And then upon the grass I sit, and moan,
'Like one who once had wings.—O why should I
'Feel curs'd and thwarted, when the liegeless air
'Yields to my step aspirant? why should I
'Spurn the green turf as hateful to my feet?
95 'Goddess benign, point forth some unknown thing:

105   *alarum* – commotion.

115   *sovran* – sovereign.

119   *elixir* – a liquor or potion which was once supposed to prolong life
       indefinitely.
120   *the God* – as a result of gazing closely at Mnemosyne's face, Apollo
       gains great knowledge and insight and is reborn as a god.

'Are there not other regions than this isle?
'What are the stars? There is the sun, the sun!
'And the most patient brillance of the moon!
'And stars by thousands! Point me out the way
100 'To any one particular beauteous star,
'And I will flit into it with my lyre,
'And make its silvery splendour pant with bliss.
'I have heard the cloudy thunder: Where is power?
'Whose hand, whose essence, what divinity
105 'Makes this alarum in the elements,
'While I here idle listen on the shores
'In fearless yet in aching ignorance?
'O tell me, lonely Goddess, by thy harp
'That waileth every morn and eventide,
110 'Tell me why thus I rave, about these groves!
'Mute thou remainest—Mute! yet I can read
'A wondrous lesson in thy silent face:
'Knowledge enormous makes a God of me.
'Names, deeds, gray legends, dire events, rebellions,
115 'Majesties, sovran voices, agonies,
'Creations and destroyings, all at once
'Pour into the wide hollows of my brain,
'And deify me, as if some blithe wine
'Or bright elixir peerless I had drunk,
120 'And so become immortal.'—Thus the God,
While his enkindled eyes, with level glance
Beneath his white soft temples, stedfast kept
Trembling with light upon Mnemosyne.
Soon wild commotions shook him, and made flush
125 All the immortal fairness of his limbs;
Most like the struggle at the gate of death;
Or liker still to one who should take leave
Of pale immortal death, and with a pang
As hot as death's is chill, with fierce convulse
130 Die into life: so young Apollo anguish'd:

The narrative breaks off in mid-sentence. It is generally accepted that Keats abandoned this poem when his brother, Tom, died.

To James Augustus Hessey, 8 October 1818

James Hessey, working with James Taylor, ran the firm which published Keats's poems.

2 *Chronicle* – The **London Morning Chronicle;** J.S. (John Scott) had written a letter defending Keats against Crocker's attack on *Endymion* in the **Quarterly Review.**

His very hair, his golden tresses famed
Kept undulation round his eager neck.
During the pain Mnemosyne upheld
Her arms as one who prophesied.—At length
135   Apollo shriek'd;—and lo! from all his limbs
Celestial...

To JAMES AUGUSTUS HESSEY
[Thursday 8 Oct. 1818]
My dear Hessey,

    You are very good in sending me the letter from the Chronicle—
and I am very bad in not acknowledging such a kindness sooner.—
pray forgive me.—It has so chanced that I have had that paper
5 every day—I have seen today's. I cannot but feel indebted to those
Gentlemen who have taken my part—As for the rest, I begin to get
a little acquainted with my own strength and weakness.—Praise
or blame has but a momentary effect on the man whose love of
beauty in the abstract makes him a severe critic on his own Works.
10 My own domestic criticism has given me pain without comparison
beyond what Blackwood or the Quarterly could possibly inflict.
And also when I feel I am right no external praise can give me such
a glow as my own solitary reperception & ratification of what is
fine. J.S. is perfectly right in regard to the slip-shod Endymion.
15 That it is so is no fault of mine.—No!—though it may sound a little
paradoxical. It is as good as I had power to make it—by myself—
Had I been nervous about its being a perfect piece, & with that
view asked advice, & trembled over every page, it would not have
been written; for it is not in my nature to fumble—I will write
20 independantly.—I have written independently without Judgment.—I may write independently, & *with judgment* hereafter.—
The Genius of Poetry must work out its own salvation in a man: It
cannot be matured by law & precept, but by sensation & watchful-
ness in itself. That which is creative must create itself—In
25 Endymion, I leaped headlong into the Sea, and thereby have

become better acquainted with the Soundings, the quicksands, & the rocks, than if I had stayed upon the green shore, and piped a silly pipe, and took tea & comfortable advice.—I was never afraid of failure; for I would sooner fail than not be among the greatest—

30 But I am nigh getting into a rant. So, with remembrances to Taylor and Woodhouse &c I am

Yrs very sincerely
John Keats.

To George and Georgiana Keats, 14 October 1818

In this extract, from a long letter to his brother and sister-in-law who were living in America, Keats describes Jane Cox whom he met when visiting the Reynolds home.

To George and Georgiana Keats, 26 October 1818

This extract was part of a long journal letter (signed off on 31 October) that Keats sent to his brother and sister-in-law in America.

1   same Lady again – a reference to Mrs Isabella Jones, known to many of Keats's friends.

To GEORGE AND GEORGIANA KEATS
[Wednesday 14] Oct. 1818

...She is not a Cleopatra; but she is at least a Charmian. She has a rich eastern look; she has fine eyes and fine manners. When she comes into a room she makes an impression the same as the Beauty of a Leopardess. She is too fine and too con[s]cious of her Self to
5   repulse any Man who may address her—from habit she thinks that nothing *particular*. I always find myself more at ease with such a woman; the picture before me always gives me a life and animation which I cannot possibly feel with anything inferiour—I am at such times too much occupied in admiring to be awkward or on a
10 tremble. I forget myself entirely because I live in her. You will by this time think I am in love with her; so before I go any further I will tell you I am not—she kept me awake one Night as a tune of Mozart's might do—I speak of the thing as a passtime and an amuzement than which I can feel none deeper than a conversation
15 with an imperial woman the very 'yes' and 'no' of whose Lips is to me a Banquet. I dont cry to take the moon home with me in my Pocket not [*for* nor] do I fret to leave her behind me. I like her and her like because one has no *sensations*—what we both are is taken for granted—

To GEORGE AND GEORGIANA KEATS
[Monday 26] Oct. 1818

....Since I wrote thus far I have met with that same Lady again, whom I saw at Hastings and whom I met when we were going to the English Opera. It was in a street which goes from Bedford Row to Lamb's Conduit Street—I passed her and turned back—she
5   seemed glad of it; glad to see me and not offended at my passing her before. We walked on towards Islington where we called on a friend of her's who keeps a Boarding School. She has always been an enigma to me—she has been in a Room with you and with Reynolds and wishes we should be acquainted without any of our

10 common acquaintance knowing it. As we went along, some times through shabby, sometimes through decent Street[s] I had my guessing at work, not knowing what it would be and prepared to meet any surprise—First it ended at this House at Islington: on parting from which I pressed to attend her home. She consented,

15 and then again my thoughts were at work what it might lead to, tho' now they had received a sort of genteel hint from the Boarding School. Our Walk ended in 34 Gloucester Street, Queen Square— not exactly so for we went up stairs into her sitting room—a very tasty sort of place with Books, Pictures a bronze statue of Buona-

20 parte, Music, æolian Harp; a Parrot, a Linnet—a Case of choice Lique[u]rs &c. &c. & she behaved in the kindest manner—made me take home a Grouse for Tom's dinner—Asked for my address for the purpose of sending more game—As I had warmed with her before and kissed her—I though[t] it would be living backwards

25 not to do so again—she had a better taste: she perceived how much a thing of course it was and shrunk from it—not in a prudish way but in as I say a good taste—She cont[r]ived to disappoint me in a way which made me feel more pleasure than a simple kiss could do—she said I should please her much more if I would only press

30 her hand and go away. Whether she was in a different disposition when I saw her before—or whether I have in fancy wrong'd her I cannot tell—I expect to pass some pleasant hours with her now and then: in which I feel I shall be of service to her in matters of knowledge and taste: if I can will—I have no libidinous thought

35 about her—she and your George are the only women à peu près de mon age whom I would be content to know for their mind and friendship alone....

To Richard Woodhouse, 27 October 1818

Here Keats is responding to a letter in which Richard Woodhouse had referred to an occasion at dinner when Keats said that he had reservations about continuing to write. Woodhouse hoped that Keats was not serious when making that comment.

27 *saturn and Ops* – characters in *Hyperion*.

To RICHARD WOODHOUSE
[Tuesday 27 Oct. 1818]
My dear Woodhouse,

Your Letter gave me a great satisfaction; more on account of its friendliness, than any relish of that matter in it which is accounted so acceptable in the 'genus irritabile'. The best answer I can give
5 you is in a clerklike manner to make some observations on two principle points, which seem to point like indices into the midst of the whole pro and con, about genius, and views and atchievements and ambition and cœtera. Ist. As to the poetical Character itself (I mean that sort of which, if I am any thing, I am a Member; that sort
10 distinguished from the wordsworthian or egotistical sublime; which is a thing per se and stands alone) it is not itself—it has no self—it is every thing and nothing—It has no character—it enjoys light and shade; it lives in gusto, be it foul or fair, high or low, rich or poor, mean or elevated—It has as much delight in conceiving an
15 Iago as an Imogen. What shocks the virtuous philosoph[h]er, delights the camelion Poet. It does no harm from its relish of the dark side of things any more than from its taste for the bright one; because they both end in speculation. A Poet is the most unpoetical of any thing in existence; because he has no Identity—he is con-
20 tinually in for—and filling some other Body—The Sun, the Moon, the Sea and Men and Women who are creatures of impulse are poetical and have about them an unchangeable attribute—the poet has none; no identity—he is certainly the most unpoetical of all God's Creatures. If then he has no self, and if I am a Poet, where is
25 the Wonder that I should say I would ~~right~~ write no more? Might I not at that very instant have been cogitating on the Characters of saturn and Ops? It is a wretched thing to confess; but is a very fact that not one word I ever utter can be taken for granted as an opinion growing out of my identical nature—how can it, when I have
30 no nature? When I am in a room with People if I ever am free from speculating on creations of my own brain, then not myself goes home to myself: but the identity of every one in the room begins to [*for* so] to press upon me that I am in a very little time an[ni]hilated—not only among Men; it would be the same in a Nursery of
35 children: I know not whether I make myself wholly understood: I hope enough so to let you see that no dependence is to be placed on what I said that day.

In the second place I will speak of my views, and of the life I purpose to myself—I am ambitious of doing the world some good:
40 if I should be spared that may be the work of maturer years—in the interval I will assay to reach to as high a summit in Poetry as the nerve bestowed upon me will suffer. The faint conceptions I have of Poems to come brings the blood frequently into my forehead— All I hope is that I may not lose all interest in human affairs—that
45 the solitary indifference I feel for applause even from the finest Spirits, will not blunt any acuteness of vision I may have. I do not think it well—I feel assured I should write from the mere yearning and fondness I have for the Beautiful even if my night's labours should be burnt every morning, and no eye ever shine upon them.
50 But even now I am perhaps not speaking from myself: but from some character in whose soul I now live. I am sure however, that this next sentence is from myself. I feel your anxiety, good opinion and friendliness in the highest degree, and am

Your's most sincerely
John Keats

> What links would you make between the content of this letter and Keats's idea of 'negative capability' as expressed in his letter of 21 December 1817?

To George and Georgiana Keats, 18 December 1818

Here Keats describes Fanny Brawne, the object of later love letters, for his brother and sister-in-law.

- 1 *Miss Brawne* – Fanny Brawne, whose family rented part of Wentworth Place, a semi-detached house on the edge of Hampstead Heath belonging to Keats's friends, Brown and Dilke.
- 2 *wants* – lacks.
- 8 *not seventeen* – Fanny Brawne was in fact eighteen but appeared younger than her age.

Ode

There are obvious links in metre and thought between this poem, written in December 1818, and *Lines on the Mermaid Tavern*. Although labelled an ode, Keats referred to this poem as 'a sort of rondeau', a short piece in which the opening lines are repeated at the end as a kind of refrain.

- 8 *parle* – conversation.

Friday [18 Dec.] 1818

....Shall I give you Miss Brawn[e]? She is about my height— with a
fine style of countenance of the lengthen'd sort—she wants senti-
ment in every feature—she manages to make her hair look well—
her nostrills are fine—though a little painful—he[r] mouth is bad
5 and good—he[r] Profil is better than her full-face which indeed is
not full put [*for* but] pale and thin without showing any bone—Her
shape is very graceful and so are her movements—her Arms are
good her hands badish—her feet tolerable—she is not seventeen—
but she is ignorant–monstrous in her behaviour flying out in all
10 directions, calling people such names—that I was forced lately to
make use of the term *Minx*–this is I think no[t] from any innate vice
but from a penchant she has for acting stylishly. I am however tired
of such style and shall decline any more of it....

Ode

Bards of Passion and of Mirth

> BARDS of Passion and of Mirth,
> Ye have left your souls on earth!
> Have ye souls in heaven too,
> Double-lived in regions new?
> 5 Yes, and those of heaven commune
> With the spheres of sun and moon;
> With the noise of fountains wond'rous,
> And the parle of voices thund'rous;
> With the whisper of heaven's trees
> 10 And one another, in soft ease

11 *Elysian* – within Elysium, the legendary home of the blessed dead.

12 *Dian* – goddess of the moon, represented as a huntress.

What effect is achieved by the rondeau form here?

Seated on Elysian lawns
Brows'd by none but Dian's fawns
Underneath large blue-bells tented,
Where the daisies are rose-scented,
15 And the rose herself has got
Perfume which on earth is not;
Where the nightingale doth sing
Not a senseless, tranced thing,
But divine melodious truth;
20 Philosophic numbers smooth;
Tales and golden histories
Of heaven and its mysteries.

    Thus ye live on high, and then
On the earth ye live again;
25 And the souls ye left behind you
Teach us, here, the way to find you,
Where your other souls are joying,
Never slumber'd, never cloying.
Here, your earth-born souls still speak
30 To mortals, of their little week;
Of their sorrows and delights;
Of their passions and their spites;
Of their glory and their shame;
What does strengthen and what maim.
35 Thus ye teach us, every day,
Wisdom, though fled far away.

    Bards of Passion and of Mirth,
Ye have left your souls on earth!
Ye have souls in heaven too,
40 Double-lived in regions new!

Fancy

In this poem, written in December 1818, Keats celebrates the pleasures of sitting by the fire and letting the imagination run free.

16 *ingle* – fire.
17 *sear faggot* – dry bundle of sticks.

21 *shoon* – shoes.

24 *Even* – evening.

28 *vassals* – servants.

Fancy

EVER let the Fancy roam,
Pleasure never is at home:
At a touch sweet Pleasure melteth,
Like to bubbles when rain pelteth;
5 Then let winged Fancy wander
Through the thought still spread beyond her:
Upon wide the mind's cage-door,
She'll dart forth, and cloudward soar
O sweet Fancy! let her loose;
10 Summer's joys are spoilt by use,
And the enjoying of the Spring
Fades as does its blossoming;
Autumn's red-lipp'd fruitage too,
Blushing through the mist and dew,
15 Cloys with tasting: What do then?
Sit thee by the ingle, when
The sear faggot blazes bright,
Spirit of a winter's night;
When the soundless earth is muffled,
20 And the caked snow is shuffled
From the ploughboy's heavy shoon;
When the Night doth meet the Noon
In a dark conspiracy
To banish Even from her sky.
25 Sit thee there, and send abroad,
With a mind self-overaw'd,
Fancy, high-commission'd:–send her!
She has vassals to attend her:
She will bring, in spite of frost,

34   *sward* – turf.

39   *quaff* – drink.

30 Beauties that the earth hath lost
   She will bring thee, all together,
   All delights of summer weather;
   All the buds and bells of May,
   From dewy sward or thorny spray
35 All the heaped Autumn's wealth,
   With a still, mysterious stealth:
   She will mix these pleasures up
   Like three fit wines in a cup,
   And thou shalt quaff it:—thou shalt hear
40 Distant harvest-carols clear;
   Rustle of the reaped corn;
   Sweet birds antheming the morn:
   And, in the same moment—hark!
   'Tis the early April lark,
45 Or the rooks, with busy caw,
   Foraging for sticks and straw.
   Thou shalt, at one glance, behold
   The daisy and the marigold;
   White-plum'd lilies, and the first
50 Hedge-grown primrose that hath burst;
   Shaded hyacinth, alway
   Sapphire queen of the mid-May;
   And every leaf, and every flower
   Pearled with the self-same shower.
55 Thou shalt see the field-mouse peep
   Meagre from its celled sleep;
   And the snake all winter-thin
   Cast on sunny bank its skin;
   Freckled nest-eggs thou shalt see
60 Hatching in the hawthorn-tree,
   When the hen-bird's wing doth rest
   Quiet on her mossy nest;
   Then the hurry and alarm
   When the bee-hive casts its swarm;

81 *Dulcet-eyed* – sweet-eyed.

81 *Ceres' daughter* – Proserpine was snatched away to the underworld by Pluto, the God of Torment (82).

85 *Hebe* – daughter of Jove, considered the personification of youth.

85 *zone* – belt.

87 *kirtle* – gown.

As you read the poem, consider how the points introduced in lines 9–15 (and later emphasized in lines 67–88) strengthen Keats's argument concerning the imagination.

65　Acorns ripe down-pattering,
　　While the autumn breezes sing.

　　　Oh, sweet Fancy! let her loose;
　　Every thing is spoilt by use:
　　Where's the cheek that doth not fade,
70　Too much gaz'd at? Where's the maid
　　Whose lip mature is ever new?
　　Where's the eye, however blue,
　　Doth not weary? Where's the face
　　One would meet in every place?
75　Where's the voice, however soft,
　　One would hear so very oft?
　　At a touch sweet Pleasure melteth
　　Like to bubbles when rain pelteth.
　　Let, then, winged Fancy find
80　Thee a mistress to thy mind:
　　Dulcet-eyed as Ceres' daughter,
　　Ere the God of Torment taught her
　　How to frown and how to chide;
　　With a waist and with a side
85　White as Hebe's, when her zone
　　Slipt its golden clasp, and down
　　Fell her kirtle to her feet,
　　While she held the goblet sweet,
　　And Jove grew languid.—Break the mesh
90　Of the Fancy's silken leash;
　　Quickly break her prison-string
　　And such joys as these she'll bring.—
　　Let the winged Fancy roam
　　Pleasure never is at home.

The Eve of St. Agnes

This poem was written early in 1819. According to superstition, a girl who goes to bed supperless on St Agnes' Eve (20 January) will have visions of her lover. The poem tells what happened to Madeline and Porphyro on that night.

4   *woolly fold* – a transferred epithet (see note to *Hyperion*, Book I, line 19).

5   *Beadsman* – a pensioner who prays for the souls of a family.

6   *rosary* – a string of beads to help his prayers.

7   *censer* – container for incense.

16   *orat'ries* – places where prayers are said.

The Eve of St. Agnes

I

ST. AGNES' EVE—Ah, bitter chill it was!
The owl, for all his feathers, was a-cold;
The hare limp'd trembling through the frozen grass,
And silent was the flock in woolly fold:
5   Numb were the Beadsman's fingers, while he told
His rosary, and while his frosted breath,
Like pious incense from a censer old,
Seem'd taking flight for heaven, without a death,
Past the sweet Virgin's picture, while his prayer he saith.

II

10   His prayer he saith, this patient, holy man;
Then takes his lamp, and riseth from his knees,
And back returneth, meagre, barefoot, wan,
Along the chapel aisle by slow degrees:
The sculptur'd dead, on each side, seem to freeze,
15   Emprison'd in black, purgatorial rails:
Knights, ladies, praying in dumb orat'ries,
He passeth by; and his weak spirit fails
To think how they may ache in icy hoods and mails.

III

Northward he turneth through a little door,
20   And scarce three steps, ere Music's golden tongue
Flatter'd to tears this aged man and poor;
But no—already had his deathbell rung;
The joys of all his life were said and sung:
His was harsh penance on St. Agnes' Eve:
25   Another way he went, and soon among

35 *cornice* – a projecting moulding along the top of a building or around a
   ceiling, sometimes 'supported' (as here) by carved angels.

37 *argent* – silver.

52 *supine* – on their backs.

Rough ashes sat he for his soul's reprieve,
And all night kept awake, for sinners' sake to grieve.

IV

That ancient Beadsman heard the prelude soft;
And so it chanc'd, for many a door was wide,
30   From hurry to and fro. Soon, up aloft,
The silver, snarling trumpets 'gan to chide:
The level chambers, ready with their pride,
Were glowing to receive a thousand guests:
The carved angels, ever eager-eyed,
35   Star'd, where upon their heads the cornice rests,
With hair blown back, and wings put cross-wise on their breasts.

V

At length burst in the argent revelry,
With plume, tiara, and all rich array,
Numerous as shadows haunting fairily
40   The brain, new stuff'd, in youth, with triumphs gay
Of old romance. These let us wish away,
And turn, sole-thoughted, to one Lady there,
Whose heart had brooded, all that wintry day,
On love, and wing'd St. Agnes' saintly care,
45   As she had heard old dames full many times declare.

VI

They told her how, upon St. Agnes' Eve,
Young virgins might have visions of delight,
And soft adorings from their loves receive
Upon the honey'd middle of the night,
50   If ceremonies due they did aright;
As, supperless to bed they must retire,
And couch supine their beauties, lily white;
Nor look behind, nor sideways, but require
Of Heaven with upward eyes for all that they desire.

58 *sweeping train* – skirts sweeping along the floor.

67 *timbrels* – tambourines.

70 *amort* – dead.

71 *lambs unshorn* – a white lamb was St. Agnes's emblem.

77 *buttress'd* – hidden in the shadow of a buttress (an external pillar or prop which supports a vertical wall).

81 *in sooth* – truly.

55   Full of this whim was thoughtful Madeline:
      The music, yearning like a God in pain,
      She scarcely heard: her maiden eyes divine,
      Fix'd on the floor, saw many a sweeping train
      Pass by—she heeded not at all: in vain
60   Came many a tiptoe, amorous cavalier,
      And back retir'd; not cool'd by high disdain,
      But she saw not: her heart was otherwhere:
    She sigh'd for Agnes' dreams, the sweetest of the year.

      She danc'd along with vague, regardless eyes,
65   Anxious her lips, her breathing quick and short:
      The hallow'd hour was near at hand: she sighs
      Amid the timbrels, and the throng'd resort
      Of whisperers in anger, or in sport;
      'Mid looks of love, defiance, hate, and scorn,
70   Hoodwink'd with faery fancy; all amort,
      Save to St. Agnes and her lambs unshorn,
    And all the bliss to be before to-morrow morn.

      So, purposing each moment to retire,
      She linger'd still. Meantime, across the moors,
75   Had come young Porphyro, with heart on fire
      For Madeline. Beside the portal doors,
      Buttress'd from moonlight, stands he, and implores
      All saints to give him sight of Madeline,
      But for one moment in the tedious hours,
80   That he might gaze and worship all unseen;
    Perchance speak, kneel, touch, kiss—in sooth such things have been.

      He ventures in: let not buzz'd whisper tell:
      All eyes be muffled, or a hundred swords

88 *lineage* – family, ancestry.

90 *beldame* – old woman.

97 *palsied* – trembling.

105 *Gossip* – old woman.

108 *bier* – stretcher or platform for supporting a corpse.

Will storm his heart, Love's fev'rous citadel:
85 For him, those chambers held barbarian hordes,
Hyena foemen, and hot-blooded lords,
Whose very dogs would execrations howl
Against his lineage: not one breast affords
Him any mercy, in that mansion foul,
90 Save one old beldame, weak in body and in soul.

XI

Ah, happy chance! the aged creature came,
Shuffling along with ivory-headed wand,
To where he stood, hid from the torch's flame,
Behind a broad hall-pillar, far beyond
95 The sound of merriment and chorus bland:
He startled her; but soon she knew his face
And grasp'd his fingers in her palsied hand,
Saying, 'Mercy, Porphyro! hie thee from this place;
'They are all here to-night, the whole blood-thirsty race!

XII

100 'Get hence! get hence! there's dwarfish Hildebrand;
'He had a fever late, and in the fit
'He cursed thee and thine, both house and land:
'Then there's that old Lord Maurice, not a whit
'More tame for his gray hairs—Alas me! flit!
105 'Flit like a ghost away.'—'Ah, Gossip dear,
'We're safe enough; here in this arm-chair sit,
'And tell me how'—'Good Saints! not here, not here;
'Follow me, child, or else these stones will be thy bier.'

XIII

He followed through a lowly arched way,
110 Brushing the cobwebs with his lofty plume,
And as she mutter'd 'Well-a—well-a-day!'
He found him in a little moonlight room,

113 *lattic'd* – with diamond-patterned window panes.

115 *holy loom . . . weaving piously* – a lambs-wool garment was woven in Rome each year on the Feast of St. Agnes.

120 *Thou must hold water in a witch's sieve . . . to venture so* – you must have used some magic spell to make you invisible.

124 *conjuror* – Madeline plans to call up (conjure) a vision of her future husband.

126 *mickle* – much (dialect).

133 *brook* – restrain.

138 *purple riot* – the blood is purple because of the speed with which it is being pumped by Porphyro's excited heart. This colour also refers to Porphyro's name which comes from the Greek for purple and is the colour associated with passion.

Pale, lattic'd, chill, and silent as a tomb.
'Now tell me where is Madeline,' said he,
115   'O tell me, Angela, by the holy loom
'Which none but secret sisterhood may see,
'When they St. Agnes' wool are weaving piously.'

XIV

'St. Agnes! Ah! it is St. Agnes' Eve—
'Yet men will murder upon holy days:
120   'Thou must hold water in a witch's sieve,
'And be liege-lord of all the Elves and Fays,
'To venture so: it fills me with amaze
'To see thee, Porphyro!—St. Agnes' Eve!
'God's help! my lady fair the conjuror plays
125   'This very night: good angels her deceive!
'But let me laugh awhile, I've mickle time to grieve.'

XV

Feebly she laugheth in the languid moon,
While Porphyro upon her face doth look,
Like puzzled urchin on an aged crone
130   Who keepeth clos'd a wond'rous riddle-book
As spectacled she sits in chimney nook.
But soon his eyes grew brilliant, when she told
His lady's purpose; and he scarce could brook
Tears, at the thought of those enchantments cold
135 And Madeline asleep in lap of legends old.

XVI

Sudden a thought came like a full-blown rose,
Flushing his brow, and in his pained heart
Made purple riot: then doth he propose
A stratagem, that makes the beldame start:
140   'A cruel man and impious thou art:
'Sweet lady, let her pray, and sleep, and dream
'Alone with her good angels far apart

143   *deem* – judge, consider.

152   *horrid* – literally, hair-raising.
153   *beard* – confront, defy.

156   *passing-bell* – the church bell tolled for a death.

158   *miss'd* – omitted, forgotten.
158   *plaining* – complaining.

162   *betide her weal or woe* – whatever the consequences for her.

171   *Merlin ... debt* – Merlin the Enchanter, magician at the court of King
       Arthur, was the son of a demon. In his old age he fell in love with a
       young woman called Nimue, who cajoled him into telling her the
       secrets of his magic power and then used one of his own spells to bury
       him alive.

'From wicked men like thee. Go, go!—I deem
'Thou canst not surely be the same that thou didst seem.'

XVII

145 'I will not harm her, by all saints I swear,'
Quoth Porphyro: 'O may I ne'er find grace
'When my weak voice shall whisper its last prayer,
'If one of her soft ringlets I displace,
'Or look with ruffian passion in her face:
150 'Good Angela, believe me by these tears;
'Or I will, even in a moment's space,
'Awake, with horrid shout, my foemen's ears,
'And beard them, though they be more fang'd than wolves and bears.'

XVIII

'Ah, why wilt thou affright a feeble soul?
155 'A poor, weak, palsy-stricken, churchyard thing,
'Whose passing-bell may ere the midnight toll;
'Whose prayers for thee, each morn and evening,
'Were never miss'd.—Thus plaining, doth she bring
A gentler speech from burning Porphyro;
160 So woful, and of such deep sorrowing,
That Angela gives promise she will do
Whatever he shall wish, betide her weal or woe.

XIX

Which was, to lead him, in close secrecy,
Even to Madeline's chamber, and there hide
165 Him in a closet, of such privacy
That he might see her beauty unespied,
And win perhaps that night a peerless bride,
While legion'd fairies pac'd the coverlet
And pale enchantment held her sleepy-eyed.
170 Never on such a night have lovers met,
Since Merlin paid his Demon all the monstrous debt.

173   *cates and dainties* – delicate and delicious food.

174   *tambour frame* – embroidery frame.

185   *fright . . . espial* – fear of being seen in (or from) the shadows. The precise sense is nicely ambiguous.

188   *amain* – greatly.

189   *agues* – shivering fits.

XX

'It shall be as thou wishest,' said the Dame:
'All cates and dainties shall be stored there
'Quickly on this feast-night: by the tambour frame
175 'Her own lute thou wilt see: no time to spare,
'For I am slow and feeble, and scarce dare
'On such a catering trust my dizzy head.
'Wait here, my child, with patience; kneel in prayer
'The while: Ah! thou must needs the lady wed,
180 'Or may I never leave my grave among the dead.'

XXI

So saying, she hobbled off with busy fear.
The lover's endless minutes slowly pass'd;
The dame return'd, and whisper'd in his ear
To follow her; with aged eyes aghast,
185 From fright of dim espial. Safe at last,
Through many a dusky gallery, they gain
The maiden's chamber, silken, hush'd, and chaste;
Where Porphyro took covert, pleas'd amain.
His poor guide hurried back with agues in her brain.

190 Her falt'ring hand upon the balustrade,
Old Angela was feeling for the stair,
When Madeline, St. Agnes' charmed maid,
Rose, like a mission'd spirit, unaware:
With silver taper's light, and pious care,
195 She turn'd, and down the aged gossip led
To a safe level matting. Now prepare,
Young Porphyro, for gazing on that bed;
She comes, she comes again, like ring-dove fray'd and fled.

XXIII

Out went the taper as she hurried in;
200 Its little smoke, in pallid moonshine, died:

206 *tongueless nightingale* – an oblique reference to the legend of Philomela, who was raped by her brother-in-law Tereus who cut out her tongue so that she could not inform against him. The gods later changed her into a nightingale.

211 *quaint device* – curious patterns.

215 *emblazonings* – devices painted on heraldic shields to identify the owner.
216 *scutcheon* – coat-of-arms.

218 *gules* – red.
219 *boon* – favour.

222 *glory* – halo.

226 *vespers* – evening prayers.

She clos'd the door, she panted, all akin
To spirits of the air, and visions wide:
No uttered syllable, or, woe betide!
But to her heart, her heart was voluble,
205   Paining with eloquence her balmy side;
As though a tongueless nightingale should swell
Her throat in vain, and die, heart-stifled, in her dell.

XXIV

A casement high and triple-arch'd there was,
All garlanded with carven imag'ries
210   Of fruits, and flowers, and bunches of knot-grass,
And diamonded with panes of quaint device,
Innumerable of stains and splendid dyes,
As are the tiger-moth's deep-damask'd wings;
And in the midst, 'mong thousand heraldries,
215   And twilight saints, and dim emblazonings,
A shielded scutcheon blush'd with blood of queens and kings.

XXV

Full on this casement shone the wintry moon,
And threw warm gules on Madeline's fair breast,
As down she knelt for heaven's grace and boon;
220   Rose-bloom fell on her hands, together prest,
And on her silver cross soft amethyst,
And on her hair a glory, like a saint:
She seem'd a splendid angel, newly drest,
Save wings, for heaven:—Porphyro grew faint:
225 She knelt, so pure a thing, so free from mortal taint.

XXVI

Anon his heart revives: her vespers done,
Of all its wreathed pearls her hair she frees;
Unclasps her warmed jewels one by one;
Loosens her fragrant boddice; by degrees

237 *poppied* – poppies are associated with sleep because of the soporific effects of opium.

240 *haven'd* – sheltered, protected.
241 *swart Paynims* – dark pagans.

257 *Morphean amulet* – Morpheus is god of sleep; an amulet is a magic charm. Porphyro wants to keep Madeline asleep until he has finished his preparations.

230 Her rich attire creeps rustling to her knees:
     Half-hidden, like a mermaid in sea-weed,
     Pensive awhile she dreams awake, and sees,
     In fancy, fair St. Agnes in her bed,
     But dares not look behind, or all the charm is fled.

XXVII

235 Soon, trembling in her soft and chilly nest,
     In sort of wakeful swoon, perplex'd she lay,
     Until the poppied warmth of sleep oppress'd
     Her soothed limbs, and soul fatigued away;
     Flown, like a thought, until the morrow-day;
240 Blissfully haven'd both from joy and pain;
     Clasp'd like a missal where swart Paynims pray;
     Blinded alike from sunshine and from rain,
     As though a rose should shut, and be a bud again.

XXVIII

     Stol'n to his paradise, and so entranced,
245 Porphyro gazed upon her empty dress,
     And listen'd to her breathing, if it chanced
     To wake into a slumberous tenderness;
     Which when he heard, that minute did he bless,
     And breath'd himself: then from the closet crept,
250 Noiseless as fear in a wide wilderness,
     And over the hush'd carpet, silent, stept,
     And 'tween the curtains peep'd, where, lo!—how fast she slept.

XXIX

     Then by the bed-side, where the faded moon
     Made a dim, silver twilight, soft he set
255 A table, and, half anguishe'd, threw thereon
     A cloth of woven crimson, gold, and jet:—
     O for some drowsy Morphean amulet!
     The boisterous, midnight, festive clarion,

270   *silken Samarcand* – a desert city in Asia, on the great Silk Road between China and the West.

276   *seraph* – one of the higher orders of angels.
277   *eremite* – hermit.

288   *woofed* – woven.

The kettle-drum, and far-heard clarionet,
260 Affray his ears, though but in dying tone:—
The hall door shuts again, and all the noise is gone.

XXX

And still she slept an azure-lidded sleep,
In blanched linen, smooth, and lavender'd,
While he from forth the closet brought a heap
265 Of candied apple, quince, and plum, and gourd
With jellies soother than the creamy curd,
And lucent syrops, tinct with cinnamon;
Manna and dates, in argosy transferr'd
From Fez; and spiced dainties, every one,
270 From silken Samarcand to cedar'd Lebanon.

XXXI

These delicates he heap'd with glowing hand
On golden dishes and in baskets bright
Of wreathed silver: sumptuous they stand
In the retired quiet of the night,
275 Filling the chilly room with perfume light.—
'And now, my love, my seraph fair, awake!
'Thou art my heaven, and I thine eremite:
'Open thine eyes, for meek St. Agnes' sake,
'Or shall I drowse beside thee, so my soul doth ache.'

XXXII

280 Thus whispering, his warm, unnerved arm
Sank in her pillow. Shaded was her dream
By the dusk curtains:—'twas a midnight charm
Impossible to melt as iced stream:
The lustrous salvers in the moonlight gleam;
285 Broad golden fringe upon the carpet lies:
It seem'd he never, never could redeem
From such a stedfast spell his lady's eyes;
So mus'd awhile, entoil'd in woofed phantasies.

292 *La belle dame sans mercy* – see note on Keats's poem of this name that appears on page 171.

296 *affrayed* – alarmed.

XXXIII

Awakening up, he took her hollow lute,—
290 Tumultuous,—and, in chords that tenderest be,
He play'd an ancient ditty, long since mute,
In Provence call'd, 'La belle dame sans mercy':
Close to her ear touching the melody;—
Wherewith disturb'd, she utter'd a soft moan:
295 He ceased—she panted quick—and suddenly
Her blue affrayed eyes wide open shone:
Upon his knees he sank, pale as smooth-sculptured stone.

XXXIV

Her eyes were open, but she still beheld,
Now wide awake, the vision of her sleep:
300 There was a painful change, that nigh expell'd
The blisses of her dream so pure and deep
At which fair Madeline began to weep,
And moan forth witless words with many a sigh;
While still her gaze on Porphyro would keep;
305 Who knelt, with joined hands and piteous eye,
Fearing to move or speak, she look'd so dreamingly.

XXXV

'Ah, Porphyro!' said she, 'but even now
'Thy voice was at sweet tremble in mine ear,
'Made tuneable with every sweetest vow;
310 'And those sad eyes were spiritual and clear:
'How chang'd thou art! how pallid, chill, and drear!
'Give me that voice again, my Porphyro,
'Those looks immortal, those complainings dear!
'O leave me not in this eternal woe,
315 'For if thou diest, my Love, I know not where to go.'

XXXVI

Beyond a mortal man impassion'd far
At these voluptuous accents, he arose,

325   *flaw-blown* – blown by gusts of wind.

335   *aye* – ever.
335   *vassal* – servant.
336   *vermeil* – bright red.

342   *infidel* – unbeliever.

344   *haggard* – wild, intractable.

346   *wassaillers* – revellers.

Ethereal, flush'd, and like a throbbing star
Seen mid the sapphire heaven's deep repose
320 Into her dream he melted, as the rose
Blendeth its odour with the violet,—
Solution sweet: meantime the frost-wind blows
Like Love's alarum pattering the sharp sleet
Against the window-panes; St. Agnes' moon hath set.

XXXVII

325 'Tis dark: quick pattereth the flaw-blown sleet:
'This is no dream, my bride, my Madeline!'
'Tis dark: the iced gusts still rave and beat:
'No dream, alas! alas! and woe is mine!
'Porphyro will leave me here to fade and pine.—
330 'Cruel! what traitor could thee hither bring?
'I curse not, for my heart is lost in thine
'Though thou forsakest a deceived thing;—
'A dove forlorn and lost with sick unpruned wing.'

XXXVIII

'My Madeline! sweet dreamer! lovely bride!
335 'Say, may I be for aye thy vassal blest?
'Thy beauty's shield, heart-shap'd and vermeil dyed?
'Ah, silver shrine, here will I take my rest
'After so many hours of toil and quest,
'A famish'd pilgrim,—saved by miracle.
340 'Though I have found, I will not rob thy nest
'Saving of thy sweet self; if thou think'st well
'To trust, fair Madeline, to no rude infidel.'

XXXIX

'Hark! 'tis an elfin-storm from faery land,
'Of haggard seeming, but a boon indeed:
345 'Arise—arise! the morning is at hand;—
'The bloated wassaillers will never heed:—

349 *Rhenish* – a German wine.

355 *darkling* – in the dark.

358 *arras* – tapestry, embroidered or woven wall-hanging.

366 *owns* – acknowledges.

'Let us away, my love, with happy speed;
'There are no ears to hear, or eyes to see,—
'Drown'd all in Rhenish and the sleepy mead:
350   'Awake! arise! my love, and fearless be,
'For o'er the southern moors I have a home for thee.'

XL

She hurried at his words, beset with fears,
For there were sleeping dragons all around,
At glaring watch, perhaps, with ready spears—
355   Down the wide stairs a darkling way they found.—
In all the house was heard no human sound.
A chain-droop'd lamp was flickering by each door;
The arras, rich with horseman, hawk, and hound,
Flutter'd in the besieging wind's uproar;
360   And the long carpets rose along the gusty floor.

XLI

They glide, like phantoms, into the wide hall;
Like phantoms, to the iron porch, they glide;
Where lay the Porter, in uneasy sprawl,
With a huge empty flaggon by his side:
365   The wakeful bloodhound rose and shook his hide,
But his sagacious eye an inmate owns:
By one, and one, the bolts full easy slide:—
The chains lie silent on the footworn stones;—
The key turns, and the door upon its hinges groans.

XLII

370   And they are gone: ay, ages long ago
These lovers fled away into the storm.
That night the Baron dreamt of many a woe,
And all his warrior-guests, with shade and form
Of witch, and demon, and large coffin-worm,
375   Were long be-nightmar'd. Angela the old

377   *thousand aves* – repetition of the prayer *Ave Maria*.

As you read the poem, make a note of any parallels with Shakespeare's Romeo and Juliet.

The Eve of St. Mark

This poem, written in February 1819, refers to the superstition that whoever watches all night at the church door on St Mark's Eve (24 April) is supposed to see the ghosts of those destined to die during the next year.

 1   *Sabbath-day* – Sunday.
 2   *Twice holy* – because it was a Saint's day as well as a Sunday.

10   *sedge* – rush-like plants.

12   *aguish* – shivery, cold.

16   *orat'ries* – places where prayers are said.
17   *demurest* – conspicuously modest and sober.
18   *vesper* – evening.

Died palsy-twitch'd, with meagre face deform;
The Beadsman, after thousand aves told,
For aye unsought for slept among his ashes cold.

The Eve of St. Mark

UPON a Sabbath-day it fell;
Twice holy was the Sabbath-bell,
That call'd the folk to evening prayer;
The city streets were clean and fair
5 From wholesome drench of April rains;
And, on the western window panes,
The chilly sunset faintly told
Of unmatured green vallies cold,
Of the green thorny bloomless hedge,
10 Of rivers new with spring-tide sedge,
Of primroses by shelter'd rills,
And daisies on the aguish hills,
Twice holy was the Sabbath-bell;
The silent streets were crowded well
15 With staid and pious companies,
Warm from their fire-side orat'ries;
And moving, with demurest air,
To even-song and vesper prayer.
Each arched porch, and entry low,
20 Was fill'd with patient folk and slow,
With whispers hush, and shuffling feet,
While play'd the organ loud and sweet.

The bells had ceased, the prayers begun,
And Bertha had not yet half done
25 A curious volume, patch'd and torn,
That all day long, from earliest morn,

28 *broideries* – intricate illuminations of the volume.

30–38 These lines list the images Bertha saw within the medieval illuminated manuscript she was reading.

36 *Covenantal Ark* – the sacred gold-encrusted chest containing the two stone tablets given by God to Moses (*Exodus* 25.16).

53 *plaited lawn-frill–* a pleated ruff.

Had taken captive her two eyes,
Among its golden broideries;
Perplex'd her with a thousand things,—
30 The stars of Heaven, and angels' wings,
Martyrs in a fiery blaze,
Azure saints in silver rays,
Aaron's breastplate, and the seven
Candlesticks John saw in Heaven,
35 The winged Lion of Saint Mark,
And the Covenantal Ark,
With its many mysteries,
Cherubim and golden mice.

Bertha was a maiden fair,
40 Dwelling in the old Minster-square;
From her fire-side she could see,
Sidelong, its rich antiquity,
Far as the Bishop's garden-wall;
Where sycamores and elm-trees tall,
45 Full-leaved, the forest had outstript,
By no sharp north-wind ever nipt,
So shelter'd by the mighty pile.
Bertha arose, and read awhile,
With forehead 'gainst the window-pane.
50 Again she tried, and then again,
Until the dusk eve left her dark
Upon the legend of St Mark.
From plaited lawn-frill, fine and thin,
She lifted up her soft warm chin,
55 With aching neck and swimming eyes,
And dazed with saintly imag'ries.

All was gloom, and silent all,
Save now and then the still foot-fall
Of one returning homewards late,
60 Past the echoing minster-gate.

61   *daws* – jackdaws.

77   *winter screen* – a protection against draughts.

79–82   These lines list the strange creatures that feature on Bertha's screen.

81   *Av'davat* – the avadavat or amadavat, an Indian songbird named after Ahmadabad, the city from which the birds were exported to Europe.

93   *eremite* – hermit.

The clamorous daws, that all the day
Above tree-tops and towers play,
Pair by pair had gone to rest,
Each in its ancient belfry-nest,
65 Where asleep they fall betimes,
To music of the drowsy chimes.

All was silent, all was gloom,
Abroad and in the homely room:
Down she sat, poor cheated soul!
70 And struck a lamp from the dismal coal;
Leaned forward, with bright drooping hair
And slant book, full against the glare.
Her shadow in uneasy guise,
Hover'd about, a giant size,
75 On ceiling-beam and old oak chair,
The parrot's cage, and panel square;
And the warm angled winter screen,
On which were many monsters seen,
Call'd doves of Siam, Lima mice,
80 And legless birds of Paradise,
Macaw, and tender Av'davat,
And silken-furr'd Angora cat.
Untired she read, her shadow still
Glower'd about, as it would fill
85 The room with wildest forms and shades,
As though some ghostly queen of spades
Had come to mock behind her back,
And dance, and ruffle her garments black.
Untired she read the legend page,
90 Of holy Mark, from youth to age,
On land, on sea, in pagan chains,
Rejoicing for his many pains.
Sometimes the learned eremite,

98   *parcell'd out* – divided up.

99–131   Keats presents these lines in fake medieval language, as if quoted from the text that Bertha is reading. Reading the lines aloud may help your understanding here. Some of the words are glossed for you below. The details outline the superstition connected with St. Mark's Eve as described on p.156.

107   *carle* – peasant, commoner.

108   *parle* – peril.

113   *everichon* – everyone.

115   *swevenis* – dreams.

121   *modre* – mother.

123   *croce* – cross.

128   *Somdel* – something.

With golden star, or dagger bright,
95   Referr'd to pious poesies
Written in smallest crow-quill size
Beneath the text; and thus the rhyme
Was parcell'd out from time to time:
'Gif ye wol stonden hardie wight—
100 Amiddes of the blacke night—
Righte in the churche porch, pardie
Ye wol behold a companie
Approuchen thee full dolourouse
For sooth to sain from everich house
105 Be it in City or village
Wol come the Phantom and image
Of ilka gent and ilka carle
Whom coldè Deathe hath in parle
And wol some day that very year
110 Touchen with foulè venime speare
And sadly do them all to die—
Hem all shalt thou see verilie—
And everichon shall by the[e] pass
All who must die that year Alas'
115 —'Als writith he of swevenis,
Men han beforne they wake in bliss,
Whanne that hir friendes thinke hem bound
In crimped shroude farre under grounde;
And how a litling child mote be
120 A saint er its nativitie,
Gif that the modre (God her blesse!)
Kepen in solitarinesse,
And kissen devoute the holy croce.
Of Goddes love, and Sathan's force,—
125 He writith; and thinges many mo:
Of swiche thinges I may not show.
Bot I must tellen verilie
Somdel of Saintè Cicilie,

134 *Exalt* – raised high.

135 *At Venice* – traditionally the burial-place of St. Mark.

To George and Georgiana Keats, 19 March 1819

Part of a long journal letter to his brother and sister-in-law in America.

2 *three figures on a greek vase* – the image of these three figures provides the basis for *Ode on Indolence*.

5 *Haslam* – William Haslam, the solicitor who was a loyal friend to Keats.

And chieflie what he auctorethe
130 Of Saintè Markis life and dethe:'

At length her constant eyelids come
Upon the fervent martyrdom;
Then lastly to his holy shrine,
Exalt amid the tapers' shine
135 At Venice,—

To GEORGE AND GEORGIANA KEATS
Friday 19 March 1819

...Neither Poetry, nor Ambition, nor Love have any alertness of
countenance as they pass by me: they seem rather like three figures
on a greek vase—a Man and two women—whom no one but myself could distinguish in their disguisement. I have this moment
5   received a note from Haslam in which he expects the death of his
Father who has been for some time in a state of insensibility—his
mother bears up he says very well—I shall go to town tommorow
to see him. This is the world—thus we cannot expect to give way
many hours to pleasure—Circumstances are like Clouds continu-
10 ally gathering and bursting—While we are laughing the seed of
some trouble is put into the wide arable land of events—while we
are laughing it sprouts is [*for* it] grows and suddenly bears a poison
fruit which we must pluck—Even so we have leisure to reason on
the misfortunes of our friends; our own touch us too nearly for
15 words. Very few men have ever arrived at a complete disinterestedness of Mind: very few have been influenced by a pure desire of
the benefit of others—in the greater part of the Benefactors of & to
Humanity some meretricious motive has sullied their greatness—
some melodramatic scenery has fa[s]cinated them—From the
20 manner in which I feel Haslam's misfortune I perceive how far I
am from any humble standard of disinterestedness—Yet this feeling ought to be carried to its highest pitch as there is no fear of its
ever injuring society—which it would do I fear pushed to an extremity—For in wild nature the Hawk would loose his Breakfast

25   of Robins and the Robin his of Worms. The Lion must starve as
      well as the swallow—The greater part of Men make their way with
      the same instinctiveness, the same unwandering eye from their
      purposes, the same animal eagerness as the Hawk—The Hawk
      wants a Mate, so does the Man—look at them both they set about
30   it and procure on[e] in the same manner—They want both a nest
      and they both set about one in the same manner—they get their
      food in the same manner—The noble animal Man for his amuse-
      ment smokes his pipe—the Hawk balances about the Clouds—that
      is the only difference of their leisures. That it is that makes the
35   Amusement of Life—to a speculative Mind. I go among the Feilds
      and catch a glimpse of a stoat or a fieldmouse peeping out of the
      withered grass—the creature hath a purpose and its eyes are bright
      with it—I go amongst the buildings of a city and I see a Man hur-
      rying along—to what? the Creature has a purpose and his eyes are
40   bright with it. But then as Wordsworth says, "we have all one
      human heart"—there is an ellectric fire in human nature tending
      to purify—so that among these human creature[s] there is con-
      tinu[a]lly some birth of new heroism—The pity is that we must
      wonder at it: as we should at finding a pearl in rubbish—I have no
45   doubt that thousands of people never heard of have had hearts
      comp[l]etely disinterested: I can remember but two—Socrates and

40 *We have all one human heart* – from Wordsworth's *'The Old Cumberland Beggar'*.

Bright Star

In this final version of this sonnet, completed by the middle of April 1819, cold images are replaced by erotic images in the closing lines. It has been suggested that Keats wrote this poem for Fanny Brawne, the girl whom he loved.

1   *steadfast* – unchanging; faithful.

4   *Eremite* – hermit.

6   *ablution* – cleansing.

Jesus—their Histories evince it—What I heard a little time ago, Taylor observe with respect to Socrates may be said of Jesus—That he was so great a man that though he transmitted no writing of his
50 own to posterity, we have his Mind and his sayings and his greatness handed to us by others. It is to be lamented that the history of the latter was written and revised by Men interested in the pious frauds of Religion. Yet through all this I see his splendour. Even here though I myself am pursueing the same instinctive course as
55 the veriest human animal you can think of—I am however young writing at random—straining at particles of light in the midst of a great darkness—without knowing the bearing of any one assertion of any one opinion. Yet may I not in this be free from sin? May there not be superior beings amused with any graceful, though instinc-
60 tive attitude my mind m[a]y fall into, as I am entertained with the alertness of a Stoat or the anxiety of a Deer? Though a quarrel in the streets is a thing to be hated, the energies displayed in it are fine; the commonest Man shows a grace in his quarrel—By a superior being our reasoning[s] may take the same tone—though erron-
65 eous they may be fine—This is the very thing in which consists poetry; and if so it is not so fine a thing as philosophy—For the same reason that an eagle is not so fine a thing as a truth—...

Bright Star

Final Version

> BRIGHT star! would I were steadfast as thou art—
>   Not in lone splendour hung aloft the night
> And watching, with eternal lids apart,
>   Like nature's patient, sleepless Eremite,
> 5 The moving waters at their priestlike task
>   Of pure ablution round earth's human shores,
> Or gazing on the new soft fallen mask
>   Of snow upon the mountains and the moors—

13 *Still, still* – this repetition stresses lack of movement plus a sense of continuity.

To GEORGE AND GEORGIANA KEATS
[Friday 16 April] 1819

...The fifth canto of Dante pleases me more and more—it is that one in which he meets with Paulo and Franchesca—I had passed many days in rather a low state of mind, and in the midst of them I dreamt of being in that region of Hell. The dream was one of the

5 most delightful enjoyments I ever had in my life—I floated about the whirling atmosphere as it is described with a beautiful figure to whose lips mine were joined at [*for* as] it seem'd for an age—and in the midst of all this cold and darkness I was warm—even flow-

10 ery tree tops sprung up and we rested on them sometimes with the lightness of a cloud till the wind blew us away again—I tried a Sonnet upon it—there are fourteen lines but nothing of what I felt in it—o that I could dream it every night—...

To George and Georgiana Keats, 16 April 1819

This extract introduces the sonnet *On a Dream* which follows.

On a Dream

Keats outlined in his letter of 16 April 1819 (printed above) how the details of this sonnet came to him after reading Canto V of Dante's *Inferno*, which describes Hell as a series of circles to which various sinners are sent.

1 *Hermes* – Mercury, the winged messenger of the gods.

2 *lulled Argus* – according to legend, Argus, the hundred-eyed giant, was lulled to sleep by Hermes' playing of the lyre.

3 *Delphic* – of Delphi, the chief shrine of Apollo, god of music.

3 *spright* – spirit.

5 *hundred eyes* – a reference back to Argus; see line 2.

7 *Ida* – mountain in Greece where Paris gave a prize for beauty to Venus, goddess of love.

8 *Tempe* – a Greek valley renowned for its landscape.

8 *Jove* – Jupiter, the most powerful of the gods; it was he who instructed Hermes to lull Argus to sleep in order to kill him.

10 *flaw* – gust.

No—yet still steadfast, still unchangeable,
10   Pillow'd upon my fair love's ripening breast,
To feel for ever its soft fall and swell,
    Awake for ever in a sweet unrest,
Still, still to hear her tender-taken breath,
    And so live ever—or else swoon to death.

On a Dream

AS Hermes once took to his feathers light,
    When lulled Argus, baffled, swoon'd and slept,
So on a Delphic reed, my idle spright
    So play'd, so charm'd, so conquer'd, so bereft
5   The dragon-world of all its hundred eyes;
    And, seeing it asleep, so fled away,
Not to pure Ida with its snow-cold skies,
    Nor unto Tempe, where Jove griev'd that day;
But to that second circle of sad hell,
10   Where in the gust, the whirlwind, and the flaw
Of rain and hail-stones, lovers need not tell
Their sorrows—pale were the sweet lips I saw,
Pale were the lips I kiss'd, and fair the form
I floated with, about that melancholy storm.

La Belle Dame sans Merci

The title of this ballad (which translates from French as *The Beautiful Lady without Pity*) is the title of a fifteenth-century poem by Alain Chartier. See page 285 for a discussion of the way in which Keats uses ballad form here.

  1 *knight-at-arms* – a medieval soldier who would usually travel on horseback dressed in full armour.

  3 *sedge* – plant that grows in wet places.

  9 *lilly* – lily, a flower traditionally associated with purity.

13 *meads* – meadows.

18 *fragrant zone* – perfumed belt.

La Belle Dame sans Merci

I

O WHAT can ail thee, knight-at-arms,
    Alone and palely loitering?
The sedge has wither'd from the lake,
    And no birds sing.

II

5 O what can ail thee, knight-at-arms,
    So haggard and so woe-begone?
The squirrel's granary is full,
    And the harvest's done.

III

I see a lilly on thy brow,
10   With anguish moist and fever dew,
And on thy cheeks a fading rose
    Fast withereth too.

IV

I met a lady in the meads,
    Full beautiful—a faery's child,
15 Her hair was long, her foot was light,
    And her eyes were wild.

V

I made a garland for her head,
    And bracelets too, and fragrant zone;
She look'd at me as she did love,
20   And made sweet moan.

VI

I set her on my pacing steed,
    And nothing else saw all day long,
For sidelong would she bend, and sing
    A faery's song.

26 *manna* – sweet-tasting food, usually associated with the sustenance that was miraculously provided for the Israelites as they travelled through the wilderness.

29 *grot* – cave.

40 *in thrall* – captive.

41 *gloam* – dusk, twilight

45 *sojourn* – remain.

What kind of woman is the Belle Dame? Is there evidence in the poem to suggest that she has been wilfully cruel to the knight?

After reading the poem, make a list of any questions that it leaves unanswered.

25 She found me roots of relish sweet,
    And honey wild, and manna dew,
    And sure in language strange she said—
        'I love thee true'.

    She took me to her elfin grot,
30   And there she wept, and sigh'd full sore,
    And there I shut her wild wild eyes
        With kisses four.

    And there she lulled me asleep,
        And there I dream'd—Ah! woe betide!
35 The latest dream I ever dream'd
        On the cold hill side.

    I saw pale kings and princes too,
        Pale warriors, death-pale were they all;
    They cried—'La Belle Dame sans Merci
40   Hath thee in thrall!'

    I saw their starved lips in the gloam,
        With horrid warning gaped wide,
    And I awoke and found me here,
        On the cold hill's side.

45 And this is why I sojourn here,
        Alone and palely loitering,
    Though the sedge has wither'd from the lake,
        And no birds sing.

To George and Georgiana Keats, 21 April 1819

Here Keats, in contemplating the problem of pain, rejects the Christian 'vale of tears' philosophy and urges his brother and sister-in-law to consider the notion of the 'vale of Soul-making'. This focus on the nature of the soul is echoed in *Ode to Psyche*, which was also written during April 1819.

To GEORGE AND GEORGIANA KEATS
Wednesday [21 April 1819]

...The common cognomen of this world among the misguided and
superstitious is 'a vale of tears' from which we are to be redeemed
by a certain arbitrary interposition of God and taken to Heaven—
What a little circumscribe[d] straightened notion! Call the world if
5   you Please "The vale of Soul-making". Then you will find out the
use of the world (I am speaking now in the highest terms for human nature admitting it to be immortal which I will here take for
granted for the purpose of showing a thought which has struck me
concerning it) I say '*Soul making*' Soul as distinguished from an
10 Intelligence—There may be intelligences or sparks of the divinity
in millions—but they are not souls ~~the~~ till they acquire identities,
till each one is personally itself. I[n]telligences are atoms of perception—they know and they see and they are pure, in short they are
God—how then are Souls to be made? How then are these sparks
15 which are God to have identity given them—so as ever to possess
a bliss peculiar to each ones individual existence? How, but by the
medium of a world like this? This point I sincerely wish to consider
because I think it a grander system of salvation than the chrystain
religion—or rather it is a system of Spirit-creation—This is effected
20 by three grand materials acting the one upon the other for a series
of years—These three Materials are the *Intelligence*—the *human
heart* (as distinguished from intelligence or Mind) and the *World* or
Elemental space suited for the proper action of *Mind and Heart* on
each other for the purpose of forming the *Soul* or *Intelligence des-*
25 *tined to possess the sense of Identity*. I can scarcely express what I but
dimly perceive—and yet I think I perceive it—that you may judge
the more clearly I will put it in the most homely form possible—I
will call the *world* a School instituted for the purpose of teaching
little children to read—I will call the *human heart* the *horn Book* used
30 in that School—and I will call the *Child able to read, the Soul* made
from that *school* and its *hornbook*. Do you not see how necessary a
World of Pains and troubles is to school an Intelligence and make
it a soul? A Place where the heart must feel and suffer in a thousand
diverse ways! Not merely is the Heart a Hornbook, It is the Minds
35 Bible, it is the Minds experience, it is the teat from which the Mind
or intelligence sucks its identity—As various as the Lives of Men

are—so various become their Souls, and thus does God make individual beings, Souls, Identical Souls of the sparks of his own essence—This appears to me a faint sketch of a system of Salvation
40 which does not affront our reason and humanity—I am convinced
that many difficulties which christians labour under would vanish
before it—There is one wh[i]ch even now Strikes me—the Salvation of Children—In them the Spark or intelligence returns to God
without any identity—it having had no time to learn of, and be
45 altered by, the heart—or seat of the human Passions—It is pretty
generally suspected that the chr[i]stian scheme has been coppied
from the ancient persian and greek Philosophers. Why may they
not have made this simple thing even more simple for common
apprehension by introducing Mediators and Personages in the
50 same manner as in the he[a]then mythology abstractions are personified—Seriously I think it probable that this System of Soul-
making—may have been the Parent of all the more palpable and
personal Schemes of Redemption, among the Zoroastrians the
Christians and the Hindoos. For as one part of the human species
55 must have their carved Jupiter; so another part must have the palpable and named Mediatior and saviour, their Christ their Oromanes and their Vishnu—If what I have said should not be plain
enough, as I fear it may not be, I will but [*for* put] you in the place
where I began in this series of thoughts—I mean, I began by seeing
60 how man was formed by circumstances—and what are circum-

56–57 *their Oromanes and their Vishnu* – oriental deities.

Ode to Psyche

Written April 1819. According to legend, Psyche was a beautiful nymph with
whom Cupid, god of love, fell in love. In the opening stanzas of this poem
Keats laments the fact that Psyche is not worshipped in a way appropriate to
a goddess of beauty.

4 *soft-conched* – shaped like a shell but soft.

6 *winged Psyche* – the Greek word Psyche means both soul and butterfly; the
soul flies above the body just as the butterfly flies from the chrysalis.

14 *Tyrian* – purple, from the purple dye of ancient Tyre.

16 *pinions* – wings.

stances?—but touchstones of his heart— and what are touchstones? but proovings of his heart?—and what are provings of his
heart but fortifiers or alterers of his nature? and what is his altered
nature but his soul?—and what was his soul before it came into the
65 world and had These provings and alterations and perfection-
ings?—An intelligence—without Identity—and how is this Identity to be made? Through the medium of the Heart? And how is the
heart to become this Medium but in a world of Circumstances?—
There now I think what with Poetry and Theology you may thank
70 your Stars that my pen is not very long winded....

Ode to Psyche

O GODDESS! hear these tuneless numbers, wrung
    By sweet enforcement and remembrance dear,
And pardon that thy secrets should be sung
    Even into thine own soft-conched ear:
5 Surely I dreamt to-day, or did I see
    The winged Psyche with awaken'd eyes?
I wander'd in a forest thoughtlessly,
    And, on the sudden, fainting with surprise,
Saw two fair creatures, couched side by side
10   In deepest grass, beneath the whisp'ring roof
Of leaves and trembled blossoms, where there ran
      A brooklet, scarce espied:

'Mid hush'd, cool-rooted flowers, fragrant-eyed,
    Blue, silver-white, and budded Tyrian,
15 They lay calm-breathing on the bedded grass;
    Their arms embraced, and their pinions too;
    Their lips touch'd not, but had not bid adieu,
As if disjoined by soft-handed slumber,
And ready still past kisses to outnumber

20 *aurorean* – Aurora was the goddess of the dawn.

21 *winged boy* – Cupid, god of love.

25 *Olympus' faded hierarchy* – enthusiasm for worshipping the Greek gods, based on Mount Olympus, had waned by the time Psyche was added to their number.

26 *Phoebe* – goddess of the moon.

27 *Vesper* – the planet Venus, associated with love.

33 *censer* – container for incense.

37 *fond, believing lyre* – this phrase suggests the pagan priests performing music before an altar as well as the poet who was traditionally presented composing on a stringed instrument.

41 *lucent fans* – shiny wings.

50 *fane* – temple.

20   At tender eye-dawn of aurorean love:
        The winged boy I knew;
    But who wast thou, O happy, happy dove?
        His Psyche true!

    O latest born and loveliest vision far
25   Of all Olympus' faded hierarchy!
    Fairer than Phoebe's sapphire-region'd star,
        Or Vesper, amorous glow-worm of the sky;
    Fairer than these, though temple thou hast none,
        Nor altar heap'd with flowers;
30   Nor virgin-choir to make delicious moan
        Upon the midnight hours;
    No voice, no lute, no pipe, no incense sweet
        From chain-swung censer teeming;
    No shrine, no grove, no oracle, no heat
35   Of pale-mouth'd prophet dreaming.

    O brightest! though too late for antique vows,
        Too, too late for the fond believing lyre,
    When holy were the haunted forest boughs,
        Holy the air, the water, and the fire;
40   Yet even in these days so far retir'd
        From happy pieties, thy lucent fans,
        Fluttering among the faint Olympians,
    I see, and sing, by my own eyes inspired.
    So let me be thy choir, and make a moan
45   Upon the midnight hours;
    Thy voice, thy lute, thy pipe, thy incense sweet
        From swinged censer teeming;
    Thy shrine, thy grove, thy oracle, thy heat
        Of pale-mouth'd prophet dreaming.

50   Yes, I will be thy priest, and build a fane
        In some untrodden region of my mind,
    Where branched thoughts, new grown with pleasant pain,

56 *zephyrs* – gentle west winds.

57 *Dryads* – tree nymphs.

60 *wreath'd trellis of a working brain* – this image brings together a reference to
   the garden plus the brain which is doing the imagining.

62 *Fancy* – read Keats's poem of this name (p. 125) for an insight into his view
   of Fancy and the workings of the imagination.

> Some have commented that this ode is characterized by an air of calm and
> melancholy. What evidence can you find to support this statement?

Ode on Indolence

This poem, written during 1819, was not published during Keats's lifetime.

1 *three figures* – these figures are named in lines 35–40.

10 *Phidian* – Phidias was a Greek sculptor.

Instead of pines shall murmur in the wind:
Far, far around shall those dark-cluster'd trees

55   Fledge the wild-ridged mountains steep by steep;
And there by zephyrs, streams, and birds, and bees,
    The moss-lain Dryads shall be lull'd to sleep;
And in the midst of this wide quietness
A rosy sanctuary will I dress

60 With the wreath'd trellis of a working brain,
    With buds, and bells, and stars without a name,
With all the gardener Fancy e'er could feign,
    Who breeding flowers, will never breed the same:
And there shall be for thee all soft delight

65   That shadowy thought can win,
A bright torch, and a casement ope at night,
    To let the warm Love in!

Ode on Indolence

   'They toil not, neither do they spin.'

ONE morn before me were three figures seen,
With bowed necks, and joined hands, side-faced;
And one behind the other stepp'd serene,
In placid sandals, and in white robes graced;

5   They pass'd, like figures on a marble urn,
When shifted round to see the other side;
They came again; as when the urn once more
Is shifted round, the first seen shades return;
And they were strange to me, as may betide

10 With vases, to one deep in Phidian lore.

How is it, Shadows! that I knew ye not?
How came ye muffled in so hush a masque?
Was it a silent deep-disguised plot
To steal away, and leave without a task

15 My idle days? Ripe was the drowsy hour;
The blissful cloud of summer-indolence

28 *throstle's lay* – song of the thrush.

41 *wanted* – lacked.

47 *honied indolence* – this is the state that Keats longs to enjoy.

Benumb'd my eyes; my pulse grew less and less;
Pain had no sting, and pleasure's wreath no flower:
O, why did ye not melt, and leave my sense
20 Unhaunted quite of all but—nothingness?

A third time came they by;—alas! wherefore?
My sleep had been embroider'd with dim dreams;
My soul had been a lawn besprinkled o'er
With flowers, and stirring shades, and baffled beams:
25 The morn was clouded, but no shower fell,
Tho' in her lids hung the sweet tears of May;
The open casement press'd a new-leav'd vine,
Let in the budding warmth and throstle's lay;
O Shadows! 'twas a time to bid farewell!
30 Upon your skirts had fallen no tears of mine.

A third time pass'd they by, and, passing, turn'd
Each one the face a moment whiles to me;
Then faded, and to follow them I burn'd
And ached for wings because I knew the three;
35 The first was a fair Maid, and Love her name;
The second was Ambition, pale of cheek,
And ever watchful with fatigued eye;
The last, whom I love more, the more of blame
Is heap'd upon her, maiden most unmeek,—
40 I knew to be my demon Poesy.

They faded, and, forsooth! I wanted wings:
O folly! What is Love! and where is it?
And for that poor Ambition—it springs
From a man's little heart's short fever-fit;
45 For Poesy!—no,—she has not a joy,—
At least for me,—so sweet as drowsy noons,
And evenings steep'd in honied indolence;
O, for an age so shelter'd from annoy,
That I may never know how change the moons,
50 Or hear the voice of busy common-sense!

54 *pet-lamb* – in a letter written a few months after this poem was composed, Keats wrote 'I hope I am a little more of a Philosopher than I was, consequently a little less of a versifying Pet-lamb'.

> How does Keats evoke his drowsy waking-dream through the lines of this poem?

To Fanny Keats, 1 May 1819

A letter to Keats's sister from Wentworth Place, overlooking Hampstead Heath in London.

10 *one of Birkbeck's sons* – Richard Birkbeck was going to join his father who had founded the English settlement in Illinois. George Keats did not in fact join Birkbeck's settlement, but set up trade in Kentucky.

12 *nice Clergyman* – Fanny was being prepared for confirmation.

20 *Mr & Mrs Dilke* – Charles and Maria Dilke, a couple with literary interests.

So, ye three Ghosts, adieu! Ye cannot raise
My head cool-bedded in the flowery grass;
For I would not be dieted with praise,
A pet-lamb in a sentimental farce!
55 Fade softly from my eyes, and be once more
In masque-like figures on the dreamy urn;
Farewell! I yet have visions for the night,
And for the day faint visions there is store;
Vanish, ye Phantoms! from my idle spright,
60 Into the clouds, and never more return!

To FANNY KEATS
Saturday [1 May 1819]

Wentworth Place Saturday—

My dear Fanny,

If it were but six oClock in the morning I would set off to see you
today: if I should so so now I could not stop long enough for a how
d'ye do—it is so long a walk through Hornsey and Tottenham—
5 and as for Stage Coaching it besides that it is very expensive it is
like going into the Boxes by way of the pit—I cannot go out on
Sunday—but if on Monday it should promise as fair as to day I will
put on a pair of loose easy palatable boots and me rendre chez
vous—I continue increasing my letter to George to send it by one
10 of Birkbeck's sons who is going out soon—so if you will let me
have a few more lines, they will be in time—I am glad you got on
so well with Monsr. le Curè—is he a nice Clergyman—a great deal
depends upon a cock'd hat and powder—not gun powder, lord
love us, but lady-meal, violet-smooth, dainty-scented lilly-white,
15 feather-soft, wigsby-dressing, coat-collar-spoiling whisker-reach-
ing, pig-tail loving, swans down-puffing, parson-sweetening powder—I shall call in passing at the tottenham nursery and see if I can
find some seasonable plants for you. That is the nearest place—or
by our la'kin or lady kin, that is by the virgin Mary's kindred, is
20 there not a twig-manufacturer in Walthamstow? Mr & Mrs Dilke
are coming to dine with us to day—they will enjoy the country
after Westminster—O there is nothing like fine weather, and
health, and Books, and a fine country, and a contented Mind, and
Diligent habit of reading and thinking, and an amulet against the

25 ennui—and, please heaven, a little claret-wine cool out of a cellar
a mile deep—with a few or a good many ratafia cakes—a rocky
basin to bathe in, a strawberry bed to say your prayers to Flora in,
a pad nag to go you ten miles or so; two or three sensible people to
chat with; two or th[r]ee spiteful folkes to spar with; two or three
30 odd fishes to laugh at and two or three numskuls to argue with—
instead of using dumb bells on a rainy day—...

Ode to a Nightingale

Charles Brown suggested that this poem, written early in May 1819, was inspired by the song of a nightingale in Wentworth Place, London, where Keats was staying at the time.

2 *hemlock* – a poisonous plant.

3 *opiate* – a sleep-inducing mixture containing opium, the juice from a species of poppy.

4 *Lethe-wards* – towards the river of forgetfulness.

7 *Dryad* – tree nymph.

13 *Flora* – goddess of flowers.

14 *Provençal song* – song from a part of southern France.

16 *blushful Hippocrene* – red wine. The Hippocrene was a fountain sacred to the Muses.

26 *Where youth . . . dies* – possibly a reference to Tom Keats, whose death on 1 December 1818 was still fresh in Keats's memory.

Ode to a Nightingale

1

MY heart aches, and a drowsy numbness pains
    My sense, as though of hemlock I had drunk,
Or emptied some dull opiate to the drains
    One minute past, and Lethe-wards had sunk:
5 'Tis not through envy of thy happy lot,
    But being too happy in thine happiness,—
        That thou, light-winged Dryad of the trees,
           In some melodious plot
    Of beechen green, and shadows numberless,
10   Singest of summer in full-throated ease.

2

O, for a draught of vintage! that hath been
    Cool'd a long age in the deep-delved earth,
Tasting of Flora and the country green,
    Dance, and Provençal song, and sunburnt mirth!
15 O for a beaker full of the warm South,
Full of the true, the blushful Hippocrene,
        With beaded bubbles winking at the brim,
           And purple-stained mouth;
That I might drink, and leave the world unseen,
20 And with thee fade away into the forest dim:

3

Fade far away, dissolve, and quite forget
    What thou among the leaves hast never known,
The weariness, the fever, and the fret
    Here, where men sit and hear each other groan;
25 Where palsy shakes a few, sad, last gray hairs,
    Where youth grows pale, and spectre-thin, and dies;
        Where but to think is to be full of sorrow
           And leaden-eyed despairs,
Where Beauty cannot keep her lustrous eyes,
30   Or new Love pine at them beyond to-morrow.

32 *Bacchus and his pards* – Bacchus, god of wine, was often represented in a chariot drawn by leopards.

33 *viewless* – invisible.

37 *Fays* – fairies.

40 *verdurous* – consisting of thick vegetation.

46 *eglantine* – honeysuckle.

51 *Darkling* – In the dark.

60 *requiem* – funeral music. Keats knows that when he is dead the bird will go on singing although he will not be able to hear it.

4

Away! away! for I will fly to thee,
    Not charioted by Bacchus and his pards,
But on the viewless wings of Poesy,
    Though the dull brain perplexes and retards:
35 Already with thee! tender is the night,
        And haply the Queen-Moon is on her throne,
            Cluster'd around by all her starry Fays;
                But here there is no light,
        Save what from heaven is with the breezes blown
40   Through verdurous glooms and winding mossy ways.

5

I cannot see what flowers are at my feet,
    Nor what soft incense hangs upon the boughs,
But, in embalmed darkness, guess each sweet
    Wherewith the seasonable month endows
45 The grass, the thicket, and the fruit-tree wild;
        White hawthorn, and the pastoral eglantine;
            Fast fading violets cover'd up in leaves;
                And mid-May's eldest child,
        The coming musk-rose, full of dewy wine,
50   The murmurous haunt of flies on summer eves.

6

Darkling I listen; and, for many a time
    I have been half in love with easeful Death,
Call'd him soft names in many a mused rhyme,
    To take into the air my quiet breath;
55 Now more than ever seems it rich to die,
        To cease upon the midnight with no pain,
            While thou art pouring forth thy soul abroad
                In such an ecstasy!
        Still wouldst thou sing, and I have ears in vain—
60   To thy high requiem become a sod.

66   *Ruth* – in the biblical story, Ruth was forced into exile by famine.

73   *the fancy* – the imagination.

What words and phrases does Keats use in stanza 1 to emphasize the beauty of the bird's song?

It has been noted that this poem focuses more on Keats's own feelings than on the bird mentioned in the title. Do you agree?

7

Thou wast not born for death, immortal Bird!
  No hungry generations tread thee down;
The voice I hear this passing night was heard
  In ancient days by emperor and clown:
65 Perhaps the self-same song that found a path
    Through the sad heart of Ruth, when, sick for home,
      She stood in tears amid the alien corn;
        The same that oft-times hath
    Charm'd magic casements, opening on the foam
70   Of perilous seas, in faery lands forlorn.

8

Forlorn! the very word is like a bell
  To toll me back from thee to my sole self!
Adieu! the fancy cannot cheat so well
  As she is fam'd to do, deceiving elf.
75 Adieu! adieu! thy plaintive anthem fades
    Past the near meadows, over the still stream,
      Up the hill-side; and now 'tis buried deep
        In the next valley-glades:
    Was it a vision, or a waking dream?
80   Fled is that music:—Do I wake or sleep?

Ode on a Grecian Urn

This ode was written in May 1819.

1   *still* – can be read as an adjective meaning 'without movement' or as an adverb meaning 'so far'.

3   *Sylvan historian* – the urn is being adressed here as a storyteller which presents events through pictures which appear on it. 'Sylvan' means 'woodland' or 'of the woods', i.e. rural.

7   *Tempe* – a valley in Greece renowned for its landscape.

7   *Arcady* – Arcadia, an area of Greece which was home to shepherds and was described as an earthly paradise.

8   *loth* – reluctant.

10   *timbrels* – tambourines.

14   *ditties of no tone* – tunes that cannot be heard by humans.

Ode on a Grecian Urn

1

THOU still unravish'd bride of quietness,
  Thou foster-child of silence and slow time,
Sylvan historian, who canst thus express
  A flowery tale more sweetly than our rhyme:
5 What leaf-fring'd legend haunts about thy shape
  Of deities or mortals, or of both,
    In Tempe or the dales of Arcady?
  What men or gods are these? What maidens loth?
  What mad pursuit? What struggle to escape?
10   What pipes and timbrels? What wild ecstasy?

2

Heard melodies are sweet, but those unheard
  Are sweeter; therefore, ye soft pipes, play on;
Not to the sensual ear, but, more endear'd,
  Pipe to the spirit ditties of no tone:
15 Fair youth, beneath the trees, thou canst not leave
  Thy song, nor ever can those trees be bare;
    Bold Lover, never, never canst thou kiss,
  Though winning near the goal—yet, do not grieve;
  She cannot fade, though thou hast not thy bliss,
20   For ever wilt thou love, and she be fair!

3

Ah, happy, happy boughs! that cannot shed
  Your leaves, nor ever bid the Spring adieu;
And, happy melodist, unwearied,
  For ever piping songs for ever new;
25 More happy love! more happy, happy love!
  For ever warm and still to be enjoy'd,
    For ever panting, and for ever young;
  All breathing human passion far above,
  That leaves a heart high-sorrowful and cloy'd,
30   A burning forehead, and a parching tongue.

41 *Attic* – from Athens in ancient Greece.

41 *brede* – elaborate decorative border.

42 *overwrought* – added to the surface.

45 *Pastoral* – idealised life of Arcadian shepherd. (See note on line 7.)

In what way does Keats personify the urn? What characteristics does it display?

4

Who are these coming to the sacrifice?
  To what green altar, O mysterious priest,
Lead'st thou that heifer lowing at the skies,
  And all her silken flanks with garlands drest?
35 What little town by river or sea shore,
    Or mountain-built with peaceful citadel,
      Is emptied of this folk, this pious morn?
And, little town, thy streets for evermore
    Will silent be; and not a soul to tell
40   Why thou art desolate, can e'er return.

5

O Attic shape! Fair attitude! with brede
  Of marble men and maidens overwrought,
With forest branches and the trodden weed;
  Thou, silent form, dost tease us out of thought
45 As doth eternity: Cold Pastoral!
    When old age shall this generation waste,
      Thou shalt remain, in midst of other woe
Than ours, a friend to man, to whom thou say'st,
    Beauty is truth, truth beauty,—that is all
50   Ye know on earth, and all ye need to know.

Ode on Melancholy

In May/June 1819, at the time of writing this ode, Keats was reading Robert Burton's *The Anatomy of Melancholy*. In this poem Keats echoes Burton's view that anyone subject to melancholy should make the best of his moods.

1 *Lethe* – one of the rivers of Hades, the underworld. Its waters induced forgetfulness.

2 *Wolf's-bane* – a poisonous plant.

4 *nightshade* – plant with poisonous red berries.

4 *ruby grape* – refers to nightshade berries.

4 *Proserpine* – a mythological character. She was kidnapped by the god of the underworld and compelled to spend six months of each year in Hades. When she returned to the mortal world, Spring and Summer returned with her.

5 *yew-berries* – poisonous berries of the yew, a tree often associated with churchyards.

6 *beetle* – death-watch beetle.

6 *death-moth* – moth with skull-like markings.

7 *Psyche* – the Greek word for both soul and butterfly. (See note on *Ode to Psyche* (p.177) for further details.)

9 *shade* – shadow of death/ghost.

14 *shroud* – a cover for a corpse.

17 *peonies* – a shrub with large, spherical flowers.

21 *She* – Melancholy.

23 *aching Pleasure* – there is a hint of sexual pleasure here.

Ode on Melancholy

1

No, no, go not to Lethe, neither twist
    Wolf's-bane, tight-rooted, for its poisonous wine;
Nor suffer thy pale forehead to be kiss'd
    By nightshade, ruby grape of Proserpine;
5 Make not your rosary of yew-berries,
    Nor let the beetle, nor the death-moth be
      Your mournful Psyche, nor the downy owl
A partner in your sorrow's mysteries;
    For shade to shade will come too drowsily,
10   And drown the wakeful anguish of the soul.

2

But when the melancholy fit shall fall
    Sudden from heaven like a weeping cloud,
That fosters the droop-headed flowers all,
    And hides the green hill in an April shroud;
15 Then glut thy sorrow on a morning rose,
    Or on the rainbow of the salt sand-wave,
      Or on the wealth of globed peonies;
Or if thy mistress some rich anger shows,
    Emprison her soft hand, and let her rave,
20   And feed deep, deep upon her peerless eyes.

3

She dwells with Beauty—Beauty that must die;
    And Joy, whose hand is ever at his lips
Bidding adieu; and aching Pleasure nigh,
    Turning to poison while the bee-mouth sips:
25 Ay, in the very temple of Delight

30   *trophies* – memorials to triumphs in war.

Lamia

Part I

Keats wrote this poem during 1819. He found the story in Robert Burton's *The Anatomy of Melancholy*. According to legend, a lamia is a blood-sucking monster with the body of a woman. In Part I of the story Lamia assumes a human shape to seduce Lycius.

2   *Satyr* – a traditionally lustful male spirit, with the legs and hoofs of a goat.

3   *King Oberon* – king of the fairies in Shakespeare's *A Midsummer Night's Dream*.

5   *Dryads and the Fauns* – wood nymphs and creatures like satyrs (2).

7   *Hermes* – messenger of the gods, well known for his love affairs.

9   *Olympus* – a mountain which was, according to legend, the home of the Greek gods.

11   *his great summoner* – Jove.

15   *Tritons* – sea gods.

18   *meads* – meadows.

Veil'd Melancholy has her sovran shrine,
Though seen of none save him whose strenuous tongue
Can burst Joy's grape against his palate fine;
His soul shall taste the sadness of her might,
30 And be among her cloudy trophies hung.

Lamia

PART I

UPON a time, before the faery broods
Drove Nymph and Satyr from the prosperous woods,
Before King Oberon's bright diadem,
Sceptre, and mantle, clasp'd with dewy gem,
5 Frighted away the Dryads and the Fauns
From rushes green, and brakes, and cowslip'd lawns,
The ever-smitten Hermes empty left
His golden throne, bent warm on amorous theft:
From high Olympus had he stolen light,
10 On this side of Jove's clouds, to escape the sight
Of his great summoner, and made retreat
Into a forest on the shores of Crete.
For somewhere in that sacred island dwelt
A nymph, to whom all hoofed Satyrs knelt;
15 At whose white feet the languid Tritons poured
Pearls, while on land they wither'd and adored.
Fast by the springs where she to bathe was wont,
And in those meads where sometime she might haunt,
Were strewn rich gifts, unknown to any Muse,
20 Though Fancy's casket were unlock'd to choose.
Ah, what a world of love was at her feet!
So Hermes thought, and a celestial heat
Burnt from his winged heels to either ear,

46 *cirque-couchant* – lying in a circle-shaped coil.
47 *gordian* – like an intricate knot; a reference to the knot of Gordius that was eventually cut with a sword by Alexander the Great.

49 *pard* – leopard.

57 *wannish* – palish.

That from a whiteness, as the lily clear,
25 Blush'd into roses 'mid his golden hair,
Fallen in jealous curls about his shoulders bare.
From vale to vale, from wood to wood, he flew,
Breathing upon the flowers his passion new,
And wound with many a river to its head,
30 To find where this sweet nymph prepar'd her secret bed:
In vain; the sweet nymph might nowhere be found,
And so he rested, on the lonely ground,
Pensive, and full of painful jealousies
Of the Wood-Gods, and even the very trees.
35 There as he stood, he heard a mournful voice,
Such as once heard, in gentle heart, destroys
All pain but pity: thus the lone voice spake:
'When from this wreathed tomb shall I awake!
'When move in a sweet body fit for life,
40 'And love, and pleasure, and the ruddy strife
'Of hearts and lips! Ah, miserable me!'
The God, dove-footed, glided silently
Round bush and tree, soft-brushing, in his speed,
The taller grasses and full-flowering weed,
45 Until he found a palpitating snake,
Bright, and cirque-couchant in a dusky brake.

    She was a gordian shape of dazzling hue,
Vermilion-spotted, golden, green, and blue;
Striped like a zebra, freckled like a pard,
50 Eyed like a peacock, and all crimson barr'd;
And full of silver moons, that, as she breathed,
Dissolv'd, or brighter shone, or interwreathed
Their lustres with the gloomier tapestries—
So rainbow-sided, touch'd with miseries,
55 She seem'd, at once, some penanced lady elf,
Some demon's mistress, or the demon's self.
Upon her crest she wore a wannish fire

58 *Ariadne's tiar* – a constellation.

63 *Proserpine* – see note to *Ode on Melancholy*, line 4. Proserpine was abducted from Sicily.

66 *pinions* – wings.

74 *Apollo* – god of music.

78 *Phoebean dart* – sunbeam; literally an arrow shot by Phoebus, the sun god.

81 *star of Lethe* – Hermes, who guided the dead beyond Lethe, one of the rivers of the underworld.

89 *serpent rod* – a wand, entwined by two snakes, carried by Hermes.

Sprinkled with stars, like Ariadne's tiar:
Her head was serpent, but ah, bitter-sweet!
60 She had a woman's mouth with all its pearls complete:
And for her eyes: what could such eyes do there
But weep, and weep, that they were born so fair?
As Proserpine still weeps for her Sicilian air.
Her throat was serpent, but the words she spake
65 Came, as through bubbling honey, for Love's sake,
And thus; while Hermes on his pinions lay,
Like a stoop'd falcon ere he takes his prey.

'Fair Hermes, crown'd with feathers, fluttering light,
'I had a splendid dream of thee last night:
70 'I saw thee sitting, on a throne of gold,
'Among the Gods, upon Olympus old,
'The only sad one; for thou didst not hear
'The soft, lute-finger'd Muses chaunting clear,
'Nor even Apollo when he sang alone,
75 'Deaf to his throbbing throat's long, long melodious moan.
'I dreamt I saw thee, robed in purple flakes,
'Break amorous through the clouds, as morning breaks,
'And, swiftly as a bright Phoebean dart,
'Strike for the Cretan isle; and here thou art!
80 'Too gentle Hermes, hast thou found the maid?'
Whereat the star of Lethe not delay'd
His rosy eloquence, and thus inquired:
'Thou smooth-lipp'd serpent, surely high inspired!
'Thou beauteous wreath, with melancholy eyes,
85 'Possess whatever bliss thou canst devise,
'Telling me only where my nymph is fled,—
Where she doth breathe!' 'Bright planet, thou hast said,'
Return'd the snake, 'but seal with oaths, fair God!'
'I swear,' said Hermes, 'by my serpent rod,
90 'And by thine eyes, and by thy starry crown!'
Light flew his earnest words, among the blossoms blown.

103   *Silenus* – an elderly satyr.

106   *steep* – soak.

107   *syrops* – syrups; magic potions.

111   *boon* – request.

114   *psalterian* – like the music of an ancient stringed instrument.

115   *Circean* – like Circe, the enchantress.

116   *damask* – red.

119   *a youth of Corinth* – Lycius, first mentioned by name in line 168.

Then thus again the brilliance feminine:
'Too frail of heart! for this lost nymph of thine,
'Free as the air, invisibly, she strays
95 'About these thornless wilds; her pleasant days
'She tastes unseen; unseen her nimble feet
'Leave traces in the grass and flowers sweet;
'From weary tendrils, and bow'd branches green,
'She plucks the fruit unseen, she bathes unseen:
100 'And by my power is her beauty veil'd
'To keep it unaffronted, unassail'd
'By the love-glances of unlovely eyes,
'Of Satyrs, Fauns, and blear'd Silenus' sighs.
'Pale grew her immortality, for woe
105 'Of all these lovers, and she grieved so
'I took compassion on her, bade her steep
'Her hair in weird syrops, that would keep
'Her loveliness invisible, yet free
'To wander as she loves, in liberty.
110 'Thou shalt behold her, Hermes, thou alone,
'If thou wilt, as thou swearest, grant my boon!'
Then, once again, the charmed God began
An oath, and through the serpent's ears it ran
Warm, tremulous, devout, psalterian.
115 Ravish'd, she lifted her Circean head,
Blush'd a live damask, and swift-lisping said,
'I was a woman, let me have once more
'A woman's shape, and charming as before.
'I love a youth of Corinth—O the bliss!
120 'Give me my woman's form, and place me where he is.
'Stoop, Hermes, let me breathe upon thy brow,
'And thou shalt see thy sweet nymph even now.'
The God on half-shut feathers sank serene,
She breath'd upon his eyes, and swift was seen
125 Of both the guarded nymph near-smiling on the green.
It was no dream; or say a dream it was,

131 *verdure* – green vegetation, turf.

133 *Caducean charm* – spell of the caduceus, the wand carried by Hermes. (See note, line 89.)

143 *lees* – last drops, dregs.

148 *besprent* – sprinkled.

151 *sear* – dried up.

158 *brede* – See note to *Ode on a Grecian Urn*, line 41.

Real are the dreams of Gods, and smoothly pass
Their pleasures in a long immortal dream.
One warm, flush'd moment, hovering, it might seem
130 Dashed by the wood-nymph's beauty, so he burn'd;
Then, lighting on the printless verdure, turn'd
To the swoon'd serpent, and with languid arm,
Delicate, put to proof the lythe Caducean charm.
So done, upon the nymph his eyes he bent
135 Full of adoring tears and blandishment,
And towards her stept: she, like a moon in wane,
Faded before him, cower'd, nor could restrain
Her fearful sobs, self-folding like a flower
That faints into itself at evening hour:
140 But the God fostering her chilled hand,
She felt the warmth, her eyelids open'd bland,
And, like new flowers at morning song of bees,
Bloom'd, and gave up her honey to the lees.
Into the green-recessed woods they flew;
145 Not grew they pale, as mortal lovers do.

Left to herself, the serpent now began
To change; her elfin blood in madness ran,
Her mouth foam'd, and the grass, therewith besprent,
Wither'd at dew so sweet and virulent;
150 Her eyes in torture fix'd, and anguish drear,
Hot, glaz'd, and wide, with lid-lashes all sear,
Flash'd phosphor and sharp sparks, without one cooling tear.
The colours all inflam'd throughout her train,
She writh'd about, convuls'd with scarlet pain:
155 A deep volcanian yellow took the place
Of all her milder-mooned body's grace;
And, as the lava ravishes the mead,
Spoilt all her silver mail, and golden brede,
Made gloom of all her frecklings, streaks and bars,
160 Eclips'd her crescents, and lick'd up her stars;

163 *rubious-argent* – reddish silver.

174 *Corinth* – a Greek city - state and major port in the Peloponnese.
174 *Cenchreas* – Cenchreae (now Kenkri) was a town on the Isthmus of Corinth in Greece, with a harbour on the Aegean Sea.
176 *Peraean rills* – mountain springs.

179 *Cleone* – village between Corinth and Argos.

188 *Spread a green kirtle* – sat with her green skirt spread out around her.
189–190 *A virgin . . . red heart's core* – a virgin yet as knowledgeable as an experienced lover.
191 *sciential* – knowledgeable.

So that, in moments few, she was undrest
Of all her sapphires, greens, and amethyst,
And rubious-argent: of all these bereft,
Nothing but pain and ugliness were left.
165 Still shone her crown; that vanish'd, also she
Melted and disappear'd as suddenly;
And in the air, her new voice luting soft,
Cried, 'Lycius! gentle Lycius!'—Borne aloft
With the bright mists about the mountains hoar
170 These words dissolv'd: Crete's forests heard no more.

Whither fled Lamia, now a lady bright,
A full-born beauty new and exquisite?
She fled into that valley they pass o'er
Who go to Corinth from Cenchreas' shore;
175 And rested at the foot of those wild hills,
The rugged founts of the Peraean rills,
And of that other ridge whose barren back
Stretches, with all its mist and cloudy rack,
South-westward to Cleone. There she stood
180 About a young bird's flutter from a wood,
Fair, on a sloping green of mossy tread,
By a clear pool, wherein she passioned
To see herself escap'd from so sore ills,
While her robes flaunted with the daffodils.

185 Ah, happy Lycius!—for she was a maid
More beautiful than ever twisted braid,
Or sigh'd, or blush'd, or on spring-flowered lea
Spread a green kirtle to the minstrelsy:
A virgin purest lipp'd, yet in the lore
190 Of love deep learned to the red heart's core.
Not one hour old, yet of sciential brain
To unperplex bliss from its neighbour pain;

198   *unshent* – unspoilt.

204   *list* – wished.
206   *Elysium* – a place where, according to Greek mythology, souls enjoy
       complete happiness.
207   *Nereids* – sea nymphs.
208   *Thetis* – sea goddess.
209   *Bacchus* – god of wine.
211   *Pluto* – god of the underworld.
211   *palatine* – palatial.
212   *Mulciber* – Vulcan, the god of fire.
212   *piazzian* – like the columns surrounding a piazza or open square.

218   *Jove* – Jupiter, king of the gods.

223   *galley* – ship.

225   *Egina* – Aegina, an island in the Aegean Sea between Athens and
       Cenchreas.

Define their pettish limits, and estrange
Their points of contact, and swift counterchange;
195 Intrigue with the specious chaos, and dispart
Its most ambiguous atoms with sure art;
As though in Cupid's college she had spent
Sweet days a lovely graduate, still unshent,
And kept his rosy terms in idle languishment.

200 Why this fair creature chose so fairily
By the wayside to linger, we shall see;
But first 'tis fit to tell how she could muse
And dream, when in the serpent prison-house,
Of all she list, strange or magnificent:
205 How, ever, where she will'd, her spirit went;
Whether to faint Elysium, or where
Down through tress-lifting waves the Nereids fair
Wind into Thetis' bower by many a pearly stair;
Or where God Bacchus drains his cups divine,
210 Stretch'd out, at ease, beneath a glutinous pine;
Or where in Pluto's gardens palatine
Mulciber's columns gleam in far piazzian line.
And sometimes into cities she would send
Her dream, with feast and rioting to blend;
215 And once, while among mortals dreaming thus,
She saw the young Corinthian Lycius
Charioting foremost in the envious race,
Like a young Jove with calm uneager face,
And fell into a swooning love of him.
220 Now on the moth-time of that evening dim
He would return that way, as well she knew,
To Corinth from the shore; for freshly blew
The eastern soft wind, and his galley now
Grated the quaystones with her brazen prow
225 In port Cenchreas, from Egina isle
Fresh anchor'd; whether he had been awhile

236   *Platonic shades* – thoughts of Plato, a Greek philosopher.

244   *syllabling* – saying.

248   *Orpheus-like at an Eurydice* – according to legend, Orpheus failed in his attempt to save his beloved Eurydice from the underworld because he, against instructions, looked back to see if she was following him.

261   *Naiad* – water nymph.

To sacrifice to Jove, whose temple there
Waits with high marble doors for blood and incense rare.
Jove heard his vows, and better'd his desire;
230 For by some freakful chance he made retire
From his companions, and set forth to walk,
Perhaps grown wearied of their Corinth talk:
Over the solitary hills he fared,
Thoughtless at first, but ere eve's star appeared
235 His phantasy was lost, where reason fades,
In the calm'd twilight of Platonic shades.
Lamia beheld him coming, near, more near—
Close to her passing, in indifference drear,
His silent sandals swept the mossy green;
240 So neighbour'd to him, and yet so unseen
She stood: he pass'd, shut up in mysteries,
His mind wrapp'd like his mantle, while her eyes
Follow'd his steps, and her neck regal white
Turn'd—syllabling thus, 'Ah, Lycius bright,
245 'And will you leave me on the hills alone?
'Lycius, look back! and be some pity shown.'
He did; not with cold wonder fearingly,
But Orpheus-like at an Eurydice;
For so delicious were the words she sung,
250 It seem'd he had loved them a whole summer long:
And soon his eyes had drunk her beauty up,
Leaving no drop in the bewildering cup,
And still the cup was full,—while he, afraid
Lest she should vanish ere his lip had paid
255 Due adoration, thus began to adore;
Her soft look growing coy, she saw his chain so sure:
'Leave thee alone! Look back! Ah, Goddess, see
'Whether my eyes can ever turn from thee!
'For pity do not this sad heart belie—
260 'Even as thou vanishest so I shall die.
'Stay! though a Naiad of the rivers, stay!

265   *Pleiad* – one of the stars of the constellation of Pleiades.

283   *essence* – substance that divine beings are made of.

289   *Swoon'd* – fainted.

293   *amenity* – agreeableness.

'To thy far wishes will thy streams obey:
'Stay! though the greenest woods be thy domain,
'Alone they can drink up the morning rain:
265 'Though a descended Pleiad, will not one
'Of thine harmonious sisters keep in tune
'Thy spheres, and as thy silver proxy shine?
'So sweetly to these ravish'd ears of mine
'Came thy sweet greeting, that if thou shouldst fade
270 'Thy memory will waste me to a shade:—
'For pity do not melt!'—'If I should stay,'
Said Lamia, 'here, upon this floor of clay,
'And pain my steps upon these flowers too rough,
'What canst thou say or do of charm enough
275 'To dull the nice remembrance of my home?
'Thou canst not ask me with thee here to roam
'Over these hills and vales, where no joy is,—
'Empty of immortality and bliss!
'Thou art a scholar, Lycius, and must know
280 'That finer spirits cannot breathe below
'In human climes, and live: Alas! poor youth,
'What taste of purer air hast thou to soothe
'My essence? What serener palaces,
'Where I may all my many senses please,
285 'And by mysterious sleights a hundred thirsts appease?
'It cannot be—Adieu!' So said, she rose
Tiptoe with white arms spread. He, sick to lose
The amorous promise of her lone complain,
Swoon'd, murmuring of love, and pale with pain.
290 The cruel lady, without any show
Of sorrow for her tender favourite's woe,
But rather, if her eyes could brighter be,
With brighter eyes and slow amenity,
Put her new lips to his, and gave afresh
295 The life she had so tangled in her mesh:
And as he from one trance was wakening

320 *Adonian feast* – celebration of Adonis, a youth loved by Venus.

329 *Peris* – good angels.

Into another, she began to sing,
Happy in beauty, life, and love, and every thing,
A song of love, too sweet for earthly lyres,
300 While, like held breath, the stars drew in their panting fires.
And then she whisper'd in such trembling tone,
As those who, safe together met alone
For the first time through many anguish'd days,
Use other speech than looks; bidding him raise
305 His drooping head, and clear his soul of doubt,
For that she was a woman, and without
Any more subtle fluid in her veins
Than throbbing blood, and that the self-same pains
Inhabited her frail-strung heart as his.
310 And next she wonder'd how his eyes could miss
Her face so long in Corinth, where, she said,
She dwelt but half retir'd, and there had led
Days happy as the gold coin could invent
Without the aid of love; yet in content
315 Till she saw him, as once she pass'd him by,
Where 'gainst a column he leant thoughtfully
At Venus' temple porch, 'mid baskets heap'd
Of amorous herbs and flowers, newly reap'd
Late on that eve, as 'twas the night before
320 The Adonian feast; whereof she saw no more,
But wept alone those days, for why should she adore?
Lycius from death awoke into amaze,
To see her still, and singing so sweet lays;
Then from amaze into delight he fell
325 To hear her whisper woman's lore so well;
And every word she spake entic'd him on
To unperplex'd delight and pleasure known.
Let the mad poets say whate'er they please
Of the sweets of Fairies, Peris, Goddesses,
330 There is not such a treat among them all,
Haunters of cavern, lake, and waterfall,

332 *lineal* – directly descended.

333 *Pyrrha's pebbles* – according to legend, after a great flood, the world was peopled again by pebbles, thrown into the water by Pyrrha and Deucalion, which were transformed into human beings.

333 *Adam's seed* – in the Bible, Adam, as the first man, is the father of the human race.

346 *not at all surmised . . .* – Lycius, so absorbed in Lamia, was not aware that she had cast a spell to shorten their journey to Corinth.

What details are included in lines 350–61 to create a realistic picture of a night walk through a city?

As a real woman, lineal indeed
From Pyrrha's pebbles or old Adam's seed.
Thus gentle Lamia judg'd, and judg'd aright,
335 That Lycius could not love in half a fright,
So threw the goddess off, and won his heart
More pleasantly by playing woman's part,
With no more awe than what her beauty gave,
That, while it smote, still guaranteed to save.
340 Lycius to all made eloquent reply,
Marrying to every word a twinborn sigh;
And last, pointing to Corinth, ask'd her sweet,
If 'twas too far that night for her soft feet.
The way was short, for Lamia's eagerness
345 Made, by a spell, the triple league decrease
To a few paces; not at all surmised
By blinded Lycius, so in her comprized.
They pass'd the city gates, he knew not how,
So noiseless, and he never thought to know.

350 As men talk in a dream, so Corinth all,
Throughout her places imperial,
And all her populous streets and temples lewd,
Mutter'd, like tempest in the distance brew'd,
To the wide-spreaded night above her towers.
335 Men, women, rich and poor, in the cool hours,
Shuffled their sandals o'er the pavement white,
Companion'd or alone; while many a light
Flared, here and there, from wealthy festivals,
And threw their moving shadows on the walls,
360 Or found them cluster'd in the corniced shade
Of some arch'd temple door, or dusky colonnade.

Muffling his face, of greeting friends in fear,
Her fingers he press'd hard, as one came near

375 *Apollonius sage* – wise Apollonius, a philosopher also known for his magical powers.

386 *Aeolian* – like a wind harp.

394 *flitter-winged* – light-winged.

> *What hint does Keats give at the end of Part I of the unhappiness that is to follow?*

With curl'd gray beard, sharp eyes, and smooth bald crown,
365 Slow-stepp'd, and robed in philosophic gown:
Lycius shrank closer, as they met and past,
Into his mantle, adding wings to haste,
While hurried Lamia trembled: 'Ah,' said he,
'Why do you shudder, love, so ruefully?
370 'Why does your tender palm dissolve in dew?'—
'I'm wearied,' said fair Lamia: 'tell me who
'Is that old man? I cannot bring to mind
'His features:—Lycius! wherefore did you blind
'Yourself from his quick eyes?' Lycius replied,
375 'Tis Apollonius sage, my trusty guide
'And good instructor; but to-night he seems
'The ghost of folly haunting my sweet dreams.'

    While yet he spake they had arrived before
A pillar'd porch, with lofty portal door,
380 Where hung a silver lamp, whose phosphor glow
Reflected in the slabbed steps below,
Mild as a star in water; for so new,
And so unsullied was the marble hue,
So through the crystal polish, liquid fine,
385 Ran the dark veins, that none but feet divine
Could e'er have touch'd there. Sounds Æolian
Breath'd from the hinges, as the ample span
Of the wide doors disclos'd a place unknown
Sometime to any, but those two alone,
390 And a few Persian mutes, who that same year
Were seen about the markets: none knew where
They could inhabit; the most curious
Were foil'd, who watch'd to trace them to their house:
And but the flitter-winged verse must tell
395 For truth's sake, what woe afterwards befel,
'Twould humour many a heart to leave them thus,
Shut from the busy world of more incredulous.

Part II

6 *non-elect* – those who have not experienced love.

9 *clench'd* – clinched.

16 *For all this* – despite all this.

24 *tythe* – fraction (literally, a tenth).

30 *harbour'd* – took shelter, lived.

PART II

LOVE in a hut, with water and a crust,
Is—Love, forgive us!—cinders, ashes, dust;
Love in a palace is perhaps at last
More grievous torment than a hermit's fast:—
5   That is a doubtful tale from faery land,
Hard for the non-elect to understand.
Had Lycius liv'd to hand his story down,
He might have given the moral a fresh frown,
Or clench'd it quite: but too short was their bliss
10   To breed distrust and hate, that make the soft voice hiss.
Besides, there, nightly, with terrific glare,
Love, jealous grown of so complete a pair,
Hover'd and buzz'd his wings, with fearful roar,
Above the lintel of their chamber door,
15   And down the passage cast a glow upon the floor.

    For all this came a ruin: side by side
They were enthroned, in the even tide,
Upon a couch, near to a curtaining
Whose airy texture, from a golden string,
20   Floated into the room, and let appear
Unveil'd, the summer heaven, blue and clear,
Betwixt two marble shafts:—there they reposed,
Where use had made it sweet, with eyelids closed,
Saving a tythe which love still open kept,
25   That they might see each other while they almost slept;
When from the slope side of a suburb hill,
Deafening the swallow's twitter, came a thrill
Of trumpets—Lycius started—the sounds fled,
But left a thought a-buzzing in his head.
30   For the first time, since first he harbour'd in

33 *forsworn* – renounced.
34 *penetrant* – acute.

36 *empery* – empire, territory.

That purple-lined palace of sweet sin,
His spirit pass'd beyond its golden bourn
Into the noisy world almost forsworn.
The lady, every watchful, penetrant,
35 Saw this with pain, so arguing a want
Of something more, more than her empery
Of joys; and she began to moan and sigh
Because he mused beyond her, knowing well
That but a moment's thought is passion's passing bell.
40 'Why do you sigh, fair creature?' whisper'd he:
'Why do you think?' return'd she tenderly:
'You have deserted me;—where am I now?
'Not in your heart while care weighs on your brow:
'No, no, you have dismiss'd me; and I go
45 'From your breast houseless: ay, it must be so.'
He answer'd, bending to her open eyes,
Where he was mirror'd small in paradise,
'My silver planet, both of eve and morn!
'Why will you plead yourself so sad forlorn,
50 'While I am striving how to fill my heart
'With deeper crimson, and a double smart?
'How to entangle, trammel up and snare
'Your soul in mind, and labyrinth you there
'Like the hid scent in an unbudded rose?
55 'Ay, a sweet kiss—you see your mighty woes.
'My thoughts! shall I unveil them? Listen then!
'What mortal hath a prize, that other men
'May be confounded and abash'd withal,
'But lets it sometimes pace abroad majestical,
60 'And triumph, as in thee I should rejoice
'Amid the hoarse alarm of Corinth's voice.
'Let my foes choke, and my friends shout afar,
'While through the throned streets your bridal car
'Wheels round its dazzling spokes.'—The lady's cheek
65 Trembled; she nothing said, but, pale and meek,

76 *sanguineous* – suffused with blood.

79–80 *Apollo's presence . . . serpent* – according to legend, the god Apollo, when young, killed Python, a serpent.

80 *certes* – certainly.

97 *the holy rite* – the prescribed rituals and ceremonies performed at the graves of ancestors.

Arose and knelt before him, wept a rain
Of sorrows at his words; at last with pain
Beseeching him, the while his hand she wrung,
To change his purpose. He thereat was stung,
70 Perverse, with stronger fancy to reclaim
Her wild and timid nature to his aim:
Besides, for all his love, in self despite
Against his better self, he took delight
Luxurious in her sorrows, soft and new.
75 His passion, cruel grown, took on a hue
Fierce and sanguineous as 'twas possible
In one whose brow had no dark veins to swell.
Fine was the mitigated fury, like
Apollo's presence when in act to strike
80 The serpent—Ha, the serpent! certes, she
Was none. She burnt, she lov'd the tyranny,
And, all subdued, consented to the hour
When to the bridal he should lead his paramour.
Whispering in midnight silence, said the youth,
85 'Sure some sweet name thou hast, though, by my truth,
'I have not ask'd it, ever thinking thee
'Not mortal, but of heavenly progeny,
As still I do. Hast any mortal name,
'Fit appellation for this dazzling frame?
90 'Or friends or kinsfolk on the citied earth,
'To share our marriage feast and nuptial mirth?'
'I have no friends,' said Lamia, 'no, not one;
'My presence in wide Corinth hardly known:
'My parents' bones are in their dusty urns
95 'Sepulchred, where no kindled incense burns,
'Seeing all their luckless race are dead, save me,
'And I neglect the holy rite for thee.
'Even as you list invite your many guests;
'But if, as now it seems, your vision rests
100 'With any pleasure on me, do not bid

116   *misery* – Lamia is aware of the misery to come when she is found out.

118   *servitors* – servants.

124   *charm* – magic spell.

126   *plantain* – a tropical tree.

133   *Teeming* – full.

'Old Apollonius—from him keep me hid.'
Lycius, perplex'd at words so blind and blank,
Made close inquiry; from whose touch she shrank,
Feigning a sleep; and he to the dull shade
105 Of deep sleep in a moment was betray'd.

   It was the custom then to bring away
The bride from home at blushing shut of day,
Veil'd, in a chariot, heralded along
By strewn flowers, torches, and a marriage song,
110 With other pageants: but this fair unknown
Had not a friend. So being left alone,
(Lycius was gone to summon all his kin)
And knowing surely she could never win
His foolish heart from its mad pompousness,
115 She set herself, high-thoughted, how to dress
The misery in fit magnificence.
She did so, but 'tis doubtful how and whence
Came, and who were her subtle servitors.
About the halls, and to and from the doors,
120 There was a noise of wings, till in short space
The glowing banquet-room shone with wide-arched grace.
A haunting music, sole perhaps and lone
Supportress of the faery-roof, made moan
Throughout, as fearful the whole charm might fade.
125 Fresh carved cedar, mimicking a glade
Of palm and plantain, met from either side,
High in the midst, in honour of the bride:
Two palms and then two plantains, and so on,
From either side their stems branch'd one to one
130 All down the aisled place; and beneath all
There ran a stream of lamps straight on from wall to wall.
So canopied, lay an untasted feast
Teeming with odours. Lamia, regal drest,
Silently paced about, and as she went,

136 *Mission'd* – ordered, sent.

146 *rout* – crowd.

151 *amain* – in full force.

155 *demesne* – property.

160 *daft* – teased.

135   In pale contented sort of discontent,
       Mission'd her viewless servants to enrich
       The fretted splendour of each nook and niche.
       Between the tree-stems, marbled plain at first,
       Came jasper pannels; then, anon, there burst
140   Forth creeping imagery of slighter trees,
       And with the larger wove in small intricacies.
       Approving all, she faded at self-will,
       And shut the chamber up, close, hush'd and still.
       Complete and ready for the revels rude,
145   When dreadful guests would come to spoil her solitude.

       The day appear'd, and all the gossip rout.
       O senseless Lycius! Madman! wherefore flout
       The silent-blessing fate, warm cloister'd hours,
       And show to common eyes these secret bowers?
150   The herd approach'd; each guest, with busy brain,
       Arriving at the portal, gaz'd amain,
       And enter'd marveling: for they knew the street,
       Remember'd it from childhood all complete
       Without a gap, yet ne'er before had seen
155   That royal porch, that high-built fair demesne;
       So in they hurried all, maz'd, curious and keen:
       Save one, who look'd thereon with eye severe,
       And with calm-planted steps walk'd in austere;
       'Twas Apollonius: something too he laugh'd,
160   As though some knotty problem, that had daft
       His patient thought, had now begun to thaw,
       And solve and melt:—'twas just as he foresaw.

       He met within the murmurous vestibule
       His young disciple. ''Tis no common rule,
165   'Lycius,' said he, 'for uninvited guest
       'To force himself upon you, and infest
       'With an unbidden presence the bright throng
       'Of younger friends; yet must I do this wrong,

171 *mien* – expression.
172 *sophist's* – learned man's
172 *spleen* – ill-humour.

176 *censer* – container for burning incense.

185 *libbard's* – leopard's.

187 *Ceres' horn* – the horn of plenty, associated with Ceres, goddess of corn.
188 *tun* – a large barrel.

194 *meet* – appropriate.

'And you forgive me.' Lycius blush'd, and led
170 The old man through the inner doors broad-spread;
With reconciling words and courteous mien
Turning into sweet milk the sophist's spleen.

Of wealthy lustre was the banquet-room,
Fill'd with pervading brilliance and perfume:
175 Before each lucid pannel fuming stood
A censer fed with myrrh and spiced wood,
Each by a sacred tripod held aloft,
Whose slender feet wide-swerv'd upon the soft
Wool-woofed carpets: fifty wreaths of smoke
180 From fifty censers their light voyage took
To the high roof, still mimick'd as they rose
Along the mirror'd walls by twin-clouds odorous.
Twelve sphered tables, by silk seats insphered,
High as the level of a man's breast rear'd
185 On libbard's paws, upheld the heavy gold
Of cups and goblets, and the store thrice told
Of Ceres' horn, and, in huge vessels, wine
Come from the gloomy tun with merry shine.
Thus loaded with a feast the tables stood,
190 Each shrining in the midst the image of a God.

When in an antichamber every guest
Had felt the cold full sponge to pleasure press'd,
By minist'ring slaves, upon his hands and feet,
And fragrant oils with ceremony meet
195 Pour'd on his hair, they all mov'd to the feast
In white robes, and themselves in order placed
Around the silken couches, wondering
Whence all this mighty cost and blaze of wealth could spring.

Soft went the music the soft air along,
200 While fluent Greek a vowel'd undersong

210 *trammels* – restraints.

211–212 *sweet wine . . .* – wine will make heaven seem nearer.

213 *Bacchus* – god of wine.

213 *meridian height* – literally, the height of the sun at mid-day, here a reference to the quantity of wine being consumed.

217 *osier'd* – woven, like twigs of willow.

224 *willow* – tree traditionally asssociated with grief.

224 *adder's tongue* – fern with leaves that resemble the shape of a snake's tongue.

226 *thyrsus* – Bacchus' rod, entwined with vine leaves and ivy.

228 *spear-grass* – upright grass.

230 *philosophy* – here Keats was referring to what we call science.

231 *awful* – inspiring awe.

232 *woof* – weave.

234 *Philosophy will clip an Angel's wings* – Keats was known to be concerned that science was taking the wonder out of life.

What effect is achieved by the move to the present tense in line 204?

Kept up among the guests, discoursing low
At first, for scarcely was the wine at flow;
But when the happy vintage touch'd their brains,
Louder they talk, and louder come the strains
205 Of powerful instruments:—the gorgeous dyes,
The space, the splendour of the draperies,
The roof of awful richness, nectarous cheer,
Beautiful slaves, and Lamia's self, appear,
Now, when the wine has done its rosy deed,
210 And every soul from human trammels freed,
No more so strange; for merry wine, sweet wine,
Will make Elysian shades not too fair, too divine.
Soon was God Bacchus at meridian height;
Flush'd were their cheeks, and bright eyes double bright:
215 Garlands of every green, and every scent
From vales deflower'd, or forest-trees branch-rent,
In baskets of bright osier'd gold were brought
High as the handles heap'd, to suit the thought
Of every guest; that each, as he did please,
220 Might fancy-fit his brows, silk-pillow'd at his ease.

What wreath for Lamia? What for Lycius?
What for the sage, old Apollonius?
Upon her aching forehead be there hung
The leaves of willow and of adder's tongue;
225 And for the youth, quick, let us strip for him
The thyrsus, that his watching eyes may swim
Into forgetfulness; and, for the sage,
Let spear-grass and the spiteful thistle wage
War on his temples. Do not all charms fly
230 At the mere touch of cold philosophy?
There was an awful rainbow once in heaven:
We know her woof, her texture; she is given
In the dull catalogue of common things.
Philosophy will clip an Angel's wings,

236   *gnomed* – peopled or worked by gnomes.

257   *Own'd* – acknowledged.

264   *myrtle* – tree held sacred to Venus, goddess of love.

268   *And not a man . . . terror in his hair* – Everyone's hair stood on end.

235 Conquer all mysteries by rule and line,
Empty the haunted air, and gnomed mine—
Unweave a rainbow, as it erewhile made
The tender-person'd Lamia melt into a shade.

By her glad Lycius sitting, in chief place,
240 Scarce saw in all the room another face,
Till, checking his love trance, a cup he took
Full brimm'd, and opposite sent forth a look
'Cross the broad table, to beseech a glance
From his old teacher's wrinkled countenance,
245 And pledge him. The bald-head philosopher
Had fix'd his eye, without a twinkle or stir
Full on the alarmed beauty of the bride,
Brow-beating her fair form, and troubling her sweet pride.
Lycius then press'd her hand, with devout touch,
250 As pale it lay upon the rosy couch:
'Twas icy, and the cold ran through his veins:
Then sudden it grew hot, and all the pains
Of an unnatural heat shot to his heart.
'Lamia, what means this? Wherefore dost thou start?
255 'Know'st thou that man?' Poor Lamia answer'd not.
He gaz'd into her eyes, and not a jot
Own'd they the lovelorn piteous appeal:
More, more he gaz'd: his human senses reel:
Some hungry spell that loveliness absorbs;
260 There was no recognition in those orbs.
'Lamia!' he cried—and no soft-toned reply.
The many heard, and the loud revelry
Grew hush; the stately music no more breathes;
The myrtle sicken'd in a thousand wreaths.
265 By faint degrees, voice, lute, and pleasure ceased;
A deadly silence step by step increased,
Until it seem'd a horrid presence there,
And not a man but felt the terror in his hair.

285 *sophistries* – teachings of philosophy and rhetoric.

291 *sophist* – reference to Apollonius as a teacher of knowledge.

294 *supine* – lying on his back.

301 *perceant* – piercing.

'Lamia!' he shriek'd; and nothing but the shriek
With its sad echo did the silence break.
270 'Begone, foul dream!' he cried, gazing again
In the bride's face, where now no azure vein
Wander'd on fair-spaced temples; no soft bloom
Misted the cheek; no passion to illume
275 The deep-recessed vision:—all was blight;
Lamia, no longer fair, there sat a deadly white.
'Shut, shut those juggling eyes, thou ruthless man!
'Turn them aside, wretch! or the righteous ban
'Of all the Gods, whose dreadful images
280 'Here represent their shadowy presences,
'May pierce them on the sudden with the thorn
'Of painful blindness; leaving thee forlorn,
'In trembling dotage to the feeblest fright
'Of conscience, for their long offended might,
285 'For all thine impious proud-heart sophistries,
'Unlawful magic, and enticing lies.
'Corinthians! look upon that gray-beard wretch!
'Mark how, possess'd, his lashless eyelids stretch
'Around his demon eyes! Corinthians, see!
290 'My sweet bride withers at their potency.'
'Fool!' said the sophist, in an under-tone
Gruff with contempt; which a death-nighing moan
From Lycius answer'd, as heart-struck and lost,
He sank supine beside the aching ghost.
295 'Fool! Fool!' repeated he, while his eyes still
Relented not, nor mov'd; 'from every ill
'Of life have I preserv'd thee to this day,
'And shall I see thee made a serpent's prey?'
Then Lamia breath'd death breath; the sophist's eye,
300 Like a sharp spear, went through her utterly,
Keen, cruel, perceant, stinging: she, as well
As her weak hand could any meaning tell,
Motion'd him to be silent; vainly so,

> With whom do your sympathies lie after reading this poem? With Lamia – as victim or deceiver? With Lycius – as victim or tyrant? With Apollonius – as voice of reason or murderer?

To George and Georgiana Keats, 18 September 1819

1   *Dilkes* – the London home of Charles and Maria Dilke.

7   *Brown* – Charles Brown, a friend who owned part of Wentworth Place in Hampstead where Keats lived as a tenant.

13   *lauding* – praising.

He look'd and look'd again a level—No!
'A Serpent!' echoed he; no sooner said,
305 Than with a frightful scream she vanished:
And Lycius' arms were empty of delight,
As were his limbs of life, from that same night,
On the high couch he lay!—his friends came round—
Supported him—no pulse, or breath they found,
310 And, in its marriage robe, the heavy body wound.

To GEORGE AND GEORGIANA KEATS
Saturday [18 September 1819]

...A circumsta[n]ce [which] occur[r]ed lately at Dilkes—I think it
very rich and dramatic and quite illustrative of the little quiet fun
that he will enjoy sometimes. First I must tell you their house is at
the corner of Great Smith Street, so that some of the windows look
into one Street, and the back windows into another round the cor-
5 ner—Dilke had some old people to dinner, I know not who—but
there were told old ladies among them—Brown was there—they
had known him from a Child. Brown is very pleasant with old
women, and on that day, it seems, behaved himself so winningly
10 they [*for* that] they became hand and glove together and a little
complimentary. Brown was obliged to depart early. He bid them
good bye and pass'd into the passage—no sooner was his back
turned than the old women began lauding him. When Brown had
reach'd the Street door and was just going, Dilke threw up the
15 Window and call'd 'Brown! Brown! They say you look younger
than ever you did!' Brown went on and had just turn'd the corner
into the other street when Dilke appeared at the back window
crying "Brown! Brown! By God, they say you're handsome!" You
see what a many words it requires to give any identity to a thing I
20 could have told you in half a minute....

To Autumn

In his letter of 21 September 1819 (p.245) Keats describes how he composed this poem after a Sunday walk in Winchester.

3   *him* – sun.

7   *gourd* – large fleshy fruit.

18   *swath* – corn to be cut by the scythe.

19   *gleaner* – one who gathers grain left in the field after the harvest.

21   *cyder-press* – a machine for extracting juice from apples.

22   *oozings* – here presented as a noun.

To Autumn

1

SEASON of mists and mellow fruitfulness,
    Close bosom-friend of the maturing sun;
Conspiring with him how to load and bless
    With fruit the vines that round the thatch-eves run;
5 To bend with apples the moss'd cottage-trees,
    And fill all fruit with ripeness to the core;
        To swell the gourd, and plump the hazel shells
With a sweet kernel; to set budding more,
    And still more, later flowers for the bees,
10   Until they think warm days will never cease,
        For Summer has o'er-brimm'd their clammy cells.

2

Who hath not seen thee oft amid thy store?
    Sometimes whoever seeks abroad may find
Thee sitting careless on a granary floor,
15   Thy hair soft-lifted by the winnowing wind;
Or on a half-reap'd furrow sound asleep,
    Drows'd with the fume of poppies, while thy hook
        Spares the next swath and all its twined flowers:
And sometimes like a gleaner thou dost keep
20   Steady thy laden head across a brook;
        Or by a cyder-press, with patient look,
            Thou watchest the last oozings hours by hours.

28   *sallows* – willow trees.

33   *gathering swallows* – birds group in large numbers before migrating south – a reminder of winter approaching.

What details of the opening stanza emphasize autumn as a time of plenty?

How is autumn personified in his different tasks for the season?

To John Hamilton Reynolds, 21 September 1819

In this letter Keats describes the details that inspired *To Autumn* and outlines his reasons for giving up *Hyperion*.

What examples of Miltonic inversions can you find in Hyperion?

Where are the songs of Spring? Ay, where are they?
 Think not of them, thou hast thy music too,—
25 While barred clouds bloom the soft-dying day,
 And touch the stubble-plains with rosy hue;
Then in a wailful choir the small gnats mourn
 Among the river sallows, borne aloft
  Or sinking as the light wind lives or dies;
30 And full-grown lambs loud bleat from hilly bourn;
 Hedge-crickets sing; and now with treble soft
The red-breast whistles from a garden-croft;
 And gathering swallows twitter in the skies.

To JOHN HAMILTON REYNOLDS
Tuesday [21 Sept. 1819]

...How beautiful the season is now—How fine the air. A temper-
ate sharpness about it. Really, without joking, chaste weather—
Dian skies—I never lik'd stubble fields so much as now—Aye
better than the chilly green of the spring. Somehow a stubble plain
5 looks warm—in the same way that some pictures look warm—
This struck me so much in my sunday's walk that I composed upon
it. I hope you are better employed than in gaping after weather. I
have been at different times so happy as not to know what weather
it was—No I will not copy a parcel of verses. I always somehow
10 associate Chatterton with autumn. He is the purest writer in the
English Language. He has no French idiom, or particles like
Chaucer—'tis genuine English Idiom in English words. I have
given up Hyperion—there were too many Miltonic inversions in
it—Miltonic verse can not be written but in an artful or rather
15 artist's humour. I wish to give myself up to other sensations. English ought to be kept up. It may be interesting to you to pick out
some lines from Hyperion and put a mark X to the false beauty
proceeding from art, and one 11 to the true voice of feeling. Upon
my soul 'twas imagination I cannot make the distinction—Every
20 now & then there is a Miltonic intonation—But I cannot make the
division properly....

The Fall of Hyperion

These 326 lines, written in September 1819, appear at the beginning of the first canto of *The Fall of Hyperion*. (A canto – from the Italian for melody or song – refers to a section of a long poem that would be sung.) Parallels have been drawn between the structure that Keats is establishing here and Dante's *Divine Comedy*, an account of a journey through Hell, Purgatory and Paradise, also divided into cantos. In both works, the central character is guided on his journey.

The dream vision that Keats outlines in this fragment begins with a description of a lavish banquet found in the middle of a forest, then moves to a temple and an encounter with Moneta (another name for Mnemosyne) who transports the poet to the vale mentioned in the opening of *Hyperion* Book I.

10 *sable charm* – religion.

13 *clod* – lump of solid matter.

The Fall of Hyperion

A DREAM

FANATICS have their dreams, wherewith they weave
A paradise for a sect; the savage too
From forth the loftiest fashion of his sleep
Guesses at Heaven: pity these have not
5 Trac'd upon vellum or wild indian leaf
The shadows of melodious utterance.
But bare of laurel they live, dream and die;
For Poesy alone can tell her dreams,
With the fine spell of words alone can save
10 Imagination from the sable charm
And dumb enchantment. Who alive can say
'Thou art no Poet; mayst not tell thy dreams'?
Since every man whose soul is not a clod
Hath visions, and would speak, if he had lov'd
15 And been well nurtured in his mother tongue.
Whether the dream now purposed to rehearse
Be Poet's or Fanatic's will be known
When this warm scribe my hand is in the grave.
　　Methought I stood where trees of every clime,
20 Palm, myrtle, oak, and sycamore, and beech,
With Plantane, and spice blossoms, made a screen;
In neighbourhood of fountains, by the noise
Soft-showering in mine ears; and, by the touch
Of scent, not far from roses. Turning round,

27 *censers* – containers in which incense is burnt.

35 *fabled horn* – cornucopia, horn of plenty.

37 *Proserpine* – according to legend she spent half of the year in the underworld and half above ground.

42 *transparent juice* – nectar, traditionally the drink of the gods.

48 *Caliphat* – government of the Islamic world.

50 *scarlet conclave* – assembly of cardinals.

56 *Silenus* – attendant to Bacchus, the god of wine.

25 I saw an arbour with a drooping roof
   Of trellis vines, and bells, and larger blooms,
   Like floral censers swinging light in air;
   Before its wreathed doorway, on a mound
   Of moss, was spread a feast of summer fruits,
30 Which nearer seen, seem'd refuse of a meal
   By Angel tasted, or our Mother Eve;
   For empty shells were scattered on the grass,
   And grape stalks but half bare, and remnants more,
   Sweet smelling, whose pure kinds I could not know.
35 Still was more plenty than the fabled horn
   Thrice emptied could pour forth, at banqueting
   For Proserpine return'd to her own fields,
   Where the white heifers low. And appetite
   More yearning than on earth I ever felt
40 Growing within, I ate deliciously;
   And, after not long, thirsted, for thereby
   Stood a cool vessel of transparent juice,
   Sipp'd by the wander'd bee, the which I took,
   And, pledging all the Mortals of the world,
45 And all the dead whose names are in our lips,
   Drank. That full draught is parent of my theme.
   No Asian poppy, nor Elixir fine
   Of the soon fading jealous Caliphat;
   No poison gender'd in close monkish cell
50 To thin the scarlet conclave of old men,
   Could so have rapt unwilling life away.
   Amongst the fragrant husks and berries crush'd,
   Upon the grass I struggled hard against
   The domineering potion; but in vain:
55 The cloudy swoon came on, and down I sunk
   Like a Silenus on an antique vase.
   How long I slumber'd 'tis a chance to guess.
   When sense of life return'd, I started up

62 *august* – impressive, grand.

68 *superannuations* – antiquity.

75 . . . *that place the moth could not corrupt* – heaven (see *Matthew* 6.20 for the reference).

As if with wings; but the fair trees were gone,
60 The mossy mound and arbour were no more;
I look'd around upon the carved sides
Of an old sanctuary with roof august,
Builded so high, it seem'd that filmed clouds
Might spread beneath, as o'er the stars of heaven;
65 So old the place was, I remembered none
The like upon the earth: what I had seen
Of grey Cathedrals, buttress'd walls, rent towers,
The superannuations of sunk realms,
Or Nature's Rocks toil'd hard in waves and winds,
70 Seem'd but the faulture of decrepit things
To that eternal domed monument.
Upon the marble at my feet there lay
Store of strange vessels, and large draperies,
Which needs had been of dyed asbestos wove,
75 Or in that place the moth could not corrupt,
So white the linen; so, in some, distinct
Ran imageries from a sombre loom.
All in a mingled heap confus'd there lay
Robes, golden tongs, censer, and chafing dish,
80 Girdles, and chains, and holy jewelries—
    Turning from these with awe, once more I rais'd
My eyes to fathom the space every way;
The embossed roof, the silent massy range
Of columns north and south, ending in mist
85 Of nothing; then to Eastward, where black gates
Were shut against the sunrise evermore.
Then to the west I look'd, and saw far off
An Image, huge of feature as a cloud,
At level of whose feet an altar slept,
90 To be approach'd on either side by steps,
And marble balustrade, and patient travail
To count with toil the innumerable degrees.
Towards the altar sober-pac'd I went,
Repressing haste, as too unholy there;

103   *maian* – of May.

116   *gummed* – resinous (i.e. the leaves which are being burned to create incense).

125   *streams* – arteries.

95 And, coming nearer, saw beside the shrine
    One minist'ring; and there arose a flame.
    When in mid-May the sickening East Wind
    Shifts sudden to the South, the small warm rain
    Melts out the frozen incense from all flowers,
100 And fills the air with so much pleasant health
    That even the dying man forgets his shroud;
    Even so that lofty sacrificial fire,
    Sending forth maian incense, spread around
    Forgetfulness of everything but bliss,
105 And clouded all the altar with soft smoke,
    From whose white fragrant curtains thus I heard
    Language pronounc'd. 'If thou canst not ascend
    'These steps, die on that marble where thou art.
    'Thy flesh, near cousin to the common dust,
110 'Will parch for lack of nutriment—thy bones
    'Will wither in a few years, and vanish so
    'That not the quickest eye could find a grain
    'Of what thou now art on that pavement cold.
    'The sands of thy short life are spent this hour,
115 'And no hand in the universe can turn
    'Thy hour glass, if these gummed leaves be burnt
    'Ere thou canst mount up these immortal steps.'
    I heard, I look'd: two senses both at once
    So fine, so subtle, felt the tyranny
120 Of that fierce threat, and the hard task proposed.
    Prodigious seem'd the toil, the leaves were yet
    Burning,—when suddenly a palsied chill
    Struck from the paved level up to my limbs,
    And was ascending quick to put cold grasp
125 Upon those streams that pulse beside the throat:
    I shriek'd; and the sharp anguish of my shriek
    Stung my own ears—I strove hard to escape
    The numbness; strove to gain the lowest step.
    Slow, heavy, deadly was my pace: the cold

135–6   *As once fair Angels . . . heaven* – a reference to the biblical story of Jacob's dream (Genesis 28.12).

140   *choak* – choke, cut short.

144–5   *dated on/Thy doom* – postponed your death.

146   *film* – thin covering.

152   *fane* – temple.

155   *sooth* – soft, smooth. The more usual meaning of this now-obsolete word is 'truth' or 'truthful' (as in *soothsayer*).

130 Grew stifling, suffocating, at the heart;
And when I clasp'd my hands I felt them not.
One minute before death, my iced foot touch'd
The lowest stair; and as it touch'd, life seem'd
To pour in at the toes: I mounted up,
135 As once fair Angels on a ladder flew
From the green turf to heaven.—'Holy Power,'
Cried I, approaching near the horned shrine,
'What am I that should so be sav'd from death?
'What am I that another death come not
140 'To choak my utterance sacrilegious here?'
'Then said the veiled shadow—'Thou hast felt
'What 'tis to die and live again before
'Thy fated hour. That thou hadst power to do so
'Is thy own safety; thou hast dated on
145 'Thy doom,' 'High Prophetess,' said I, 'purge off
'Benign, if so it please thee, my mind's film—'
'None can usurp this height,' returned that shade,
'But those to whom the miseries of the world
'Are misery, and will not let them rest.
150 'All else who find a haven in the world,
'Where they may thoughtless sleep away their days,
'If by a chance into this fane they come,
'Rot on the pavement where thou rotted'st half—'
'Are there not thousands in the world,' said I,
155 Encourag'd by the sooth voice of the shade,
'Who love their fellows even to the death;
'Who feel the giant agony of the world;
'And more, like slaves to poor humanity,
'Labour for mortal good? I sure should see
160 'Other men here: but I am here alone.'
'They whom thou spak'st of are no vision'ries,'
Rejoin'd that voice—'they are no dreamers weak,
'They seek no wonder but the human face;
'No music but a happy-noted voice—

175 *venoms* – poisons.

183 *propitious parley* – favourable speech.

198 *Pendent* – hanging.

165　'They come out here, they have no thought to come—
　　　'And thou art here, for thou art less than they—
　　　'What benefit canst thou do, or all thy tribe,
　　　'To the great world? Thou art a dreaming thing;
　　　'A fever of thyself—think of the Earth;
170　'What bliss even in hope is there for thee?
　　　'What haven? every creature hath its home;
　　　'Every sole man hath days of joy and pain,
　　　'Whether his labours be sublime or low—
　　　'The pain alone; the joy alone; distinct:
175　'Only the dreamer venoms all his days,
　　　'Bearing more woe than all his sins deserve.
　　　'Therefore, that happiness be somewhat shar'd,
　　　'Such things as thou art are admitted oft
　　　'Into like gardens thou didst pass erewhile,
180　'And suffer'd in these Temples; for that cause
　　　'Thou standest safe beneath this statue's knees.'
　　　'That I am favored for unworthiness,
　　　'By such propitious parley medicin'd
　　　'In sickness not ignoble, I rejoice,
185　'Aye, and could weep for love of such award.'
　　　'So answer'd I, continuing, 'If it please,
　　　'Majestic shadow, tell me: sure not all
　　　'Those melodies sung into the world's ear
　　　'Are useless: sure a poet is a sage;
190　'A humanist, Physician to all men.
　　　'That I am none I feel, as Vultures feel
　　　'They are no birds when Eagles are abroad.
　　　'What am I then? Thou spakest of my tribe:
　　　'What tribe?'—The tall shade veil'd in drooping white
195　Then spake, so much more earnest, that the breath
　　　Mov'd the thin linen folds that drooping hung
　　　About a golden censer from the hand
　　　Pendent.—'Art thou not of the dreamer tribe?

200   *antipodes* – opposites.

203   *Pythia* – priestess of Apollo at Delphi, the Delphic Oracle.

222   *war* – the battle of the Titans against the Olympians.

226   *Moneta* – Mnemosyne.

229   *roofed home* – mouth.

'The poet and the dreamer are distinct,
200 'Diverse, sheer opposite, antipodes.
'The one pours out a balm upon the world,
'The other vexes it.' Then shouted I
Spite of myself, and with a Pythia's spleen,
'Apollo! faded! O far flown Apollo!

205 'Where is thy misty pestilence to creep
'Into the dwellings, thro' the door crannies,
'Of all mock lyrists, large self-worshipers,
'And careless Hectorers in proud bad verse.
'Tho' I breathe death with them it will be life
210 'To see them sprawl before me into graves.
'Majestic shadow, tell me where I am,
'Whose altar this; for whom this incense curls:
'What Image this, whose face I cannot see,
'For the broad marble knees; and who thou art,
215 'Of accent feminine, so courteous.'
Then the tall shade, in drooping linens veil'd,
Spake out, so much more earnest, that her breath
Stirr'd the thin folds of gauze that drooping hung
About a golden censer from her hand
220 Pendent; and by her voice I knew she shed
Long-treasured tears. 'This temple sad and lone
'Is all spar'd from the thunder of a war
'Foughten long since by Giant Hierarchy
'Against rebellion: this old Image here,
225 'Whose carved features wrinkled as he fell,
'Is Saturn's; I, Moneta, left supreme
'Sole priestess of his desolation.'—
I had no words to answer; for my tongue,
Useless, could find about its roofed home
230 No syllable of a fit majesty
To make rejoinder to Moneta's mourn.
There was a silence while the altar's blaze

235 *Faggots* – bundles of sticks tied together.

238 *lang'rous* – dying.

249 *sphered* – heavenly.

265 *benignant* – kindly.
266 *Soft-mitigated* – softened.

Was fainting for sweet food: I look'd thereon,
And on the paved floor, where nigh were pil'd
235 Faggots of cinnamon, and many heaps
Of other crisped spicewood—then again
I look'd upon the altar and its horns
Whiten'd with ashes, and its lang'rous flame,
And then upon the offerings again;
240 And so by turns—till sad Moneta cried,
'The sacrifice is done, but not the less,
'Will I be kind to thee for thy goodwill.
'My power, which to me is still a curse,
'Shall be to thee a wonder; for the scenes
245 'Still swooning vivid through my globed brain
'With an electral changing misery
'Thou shalt with those dull mortal eyes behold,
'Free from all pain, if wonder pain thee not.'
As near as an immortal's sphered words
250 Could to a mother's soften, were these last:
But yet I had a terror of her robes,
And chiefly of the veils, that from her brow
Hung pale, and curtain'd her in mysteries
That made my heart too small to hold its blood.
255 This saw that Goddess, and with sacred hand
Parted the veils. Then saw I a wan face,
Not pin'd by human sorrows, but bright blanch'd
By an immortal sickness which kills not;
It works a constant change, which happy death
260 Can put no end to; deathwards progressing
To no death was that visage; it had pass'd
The lily and the snow; and beyond these
I must not think now, though I saw that face—
But for her eyes I should have fled away.
265 They held me back, with a benignant light,
Soft-mitigated by divinest lids
Half-closed, and visionless entire they seem'd

288 *Omega* – the last (from the last letter of the Greek alphabet).

294 This line takes up the narrative at the point where *Hyperion* begins.

Of all external things—they saw me not,
But in blank splendor beam'd like the mild moon,
270 Who comforts those she sees not, who knows not
What eyes are upward cast. As I had found
A grain of gold upon a mountain's side,
And twing'd with avarice strain'd out my eyes
To search its sullen entrails rich with ore,
275 So at the view of sad Moneta's brow,
I ached to see what things the hollow brain
Behind enwombed: what high tragedy
In the dark secret Chambers of her skull
Was acting, that could give so dread a stress
280 To her cold lips, and fill with such a light
Her planetary eyes; and touch her voice
With such a sorrow—'Shade of Memory!'
Cried I, with act adorant at her feet,
'By all the gloom hung round thy fallen house,
285 'By this last Temple, by the golden age,
'By great Apollo, thy dear foster child,
'And by thyself, forlorn divinity,
'The pale Omega of a wither'd race,
'Let me behold, according as thou said'st,
290 'What in thy brain so ferments to and fro.'—
No sooner had this conjuration pass'd
My devout lips, than side by side we stood,
(Like a stout bramble by a solemn Pine)
Deep in the shady sadness of a vale,
295 Far sunken from the healthy breath of morn,
Far from the fiery noon and Eve's one star.
Onward I look'd beneath the gloomy boughs,
And saw, what first I thought an Image huge,
Like to the image pedestal'd so high
300 In Saturn's temple. Then Moneta's voice
Came brief upon mine ear,—'So Saturn sat
'When he had lost his realms'—Whereon there grew

303   *ken* – knowledge.

319   *margin sand* – foreshore.

What references in lines 58–136 make clear the religious setting of the poem? How would you describe the speaker's attitude towards his surroundings?

A power within me of enormous ken,
To see as a God sees, and take the depth
305 Of things as nimbly as the outward eye
Can size and shape pervade. The lofty theme
At those few words hung vast before my mind,
With half unravel'd web. I set myself
Upon an Eagle's watch, that I might see,
310 And seeing ne'er forget. No stir of life
Was in this shrouded vale, not so much air
As in the zoning of a summer's day
Robs not one light seed from the feather'd grass,
But where the dead leaf fell there did it rest.
315 A stream went voiceless by, still deaden'd more
By reason of the fallen Divinity
Spreading more shade: the Naiad 'mid her reeds
Press'd her cold finger closer to her lips.
Along the margin sand large footmarks went
320 No farther than to where old Saturn's feet
Had rested, and there slept, how long a sleep!
Degraded, cold, upon the sodden ground
His old right hand lay nerveless, listless dead,
Unsceptred; and his realmless eyes were clos'd,
325 While his bow'd head seem'd listening to the Earth,
His ancient mother, for some comfort yet.

The Cap and Bells

This poem, written during the winter of 1819–20, was the last Keats wrote; his final illness prevented him from finishing it. Although on the surface it appears to be a fairy tale in verse, it has been noted as a satire on some of the literary figures whom Keats knew. For example, in the stanzas in the extract printed here, Eban the servant has been identified as William Hazlitt, a contemporary essayist. Eban's outburst against the coachman echoes Hazlitt's attacks on literary figures of his day.

4   *The gas* – gas was introduced for lighting in London in the early nineteenth century.

18   *amain* – at full speed; without delay.
19   *string* – string which passengers pulled to signal to the driver to stop.
20   *jarvey* – coachman.
20   *hack* – a hackney cab and also the horse; literary drudge.
22   *linsey-wolsey* – a cheap textile material.

Extract from

The Cap and Bells

XXIV

IT was the time when wholesale houses close
Their shutters with a moody sense of wealth,
But retail dealers, diligent, let loose
The gas (objected to on score of health),
5   Convey'd in little solder'd pipes by stealth,
And make it flare in many a brilliant form,
That all the powers of darkness it repell'th,
Which to the oil-trade doth great scaith and harm,
And supersedeth quite the use of the glow-worm.

XXV

10   Eban, untempted by the pastry-cooks,
(Of pastry he got store within the palace),
With hasty steps, wrapp'd cloak, and solemn looks,
Incognito upon his errand sallies,
His smelling-bottle ready for the allies;
15   He pass'd the hurdy-gurdies with disdain,
Vowing he'd have them sent aboard the gallies;
Just as he made his vow, it 'gan to rain,
Therefore he call'd a coach, and bade it drive amain.

XXVI

'I'll pull the string,' said he, and further said,
20   'Polluted jarvey! Ah, thou filthy hack!
Whose springs of life are all dried up and dead,
Whose linsey-wolsey lining hangs all slack,
Whose rug is straw, whose wholeness is a crack;

27   *litter* – vehicle carrying a couch enclosed by curtains.

28   *crop* – stomach.

33   *lazar-house* – house for lepers.

35   *dowdies* – unattractively-dressed women.

37   *mien* – manner.

42   *Argus* – god with one hundred eyes; a comment on the coachman's vigilance when looking out for new custom.

44   *tilburies* – two-wheeled carriages, fashionable in the first half of the nineteenth century.

44   *phaetons* – four-wheeled open carriages.

45   *Curricles* – two-wheeled carriages, usually drawn by two horses abreast.

To Fanny Keats, 8 February 1820

Keats was taken ill on 3 February. The fever and blood-spitting of this attack clearly announced tuberculosis. His surgeon bled him and put him on a near-starvation diet. In this letter Keats describes the scene from his sickbed as he convalesces at Wentworth Place, London.

And evermore thy steps go clatter-clitter;
25   Whose glass once up can never be got back,
Who prov'st, with jolting arguments and bitter
That 'tis of modern use to travel in a litter.

XXVII

'Thou inconvenience! thou hungry crop
For all corn! thou snail-creeper to and fro,
30   Who while thou goest ever seem'st to stop,
And fiddle-faddle sandest while you go;
I' the morning, freighted with a weight of woe,
Unto some lazar-house thou journeyest,
And in the evening tak'st a double row
35   Of dowdies, for some dance or party drest,
Besides the goods meanwhile thou movest east and west.

XXVIII

'By thy ungallant bearing and sad mien
An inch appears the utmost thou couldst budge;
Yet at the slightest nod, or hint, or sign,
40   Round to the curb-stone patient dost thou trudge,
School'd in a beckon, learned in a nudge,
A dull-eyed Argus watching for a fare;
Quiet and plodding thou dost bear no grudge
To whisking tilburies, or phaetons rare,
45   Curricles, or mail-coaches, swift beyond compare.'

To FANNY KEATS
Tuesday [8 February 1820]

Wentworth Place
Tuesday morn.

My dear Fanny—

I had a slight return of fever last night, which terminated favourably, and I am now tolerably well, though weak from small quantity of food to which I am obliged to confine myself: I am sure a
5   mouse would starv[e] upon it. Mrs Wylie came yesterday. I have a very pleasant room for a sick person. A Sopha bed is made up for me in the front Parlour which looks on to the grass plot as you

remember Mrs Dilkes does. How much more comfortable than a
dull room up stairs, where one gets tired of the pattern of the bed
10   curtains. Besides I see all that passes—for instanc[e] now, this
morning, if I had been in my own room I should not have seen the
coals brought in. On sunday between the hours of twelve and one
I descried a Pot boy. I conjectured it might be the one o'Clock
beer—Old women with bobbins and red cloaks and unpresuming
15   bonnets I see creeping about the heath. Gipseys after hare skins
and silver spoons. Then goes by a fellow with a wooden clock
under his arm that strikes a hundred and more. Then comes the old
french emigrant, (who has been very well to do in france) whith his
hands joined behind on his hips, and his face full of political
20   schemes. Then passes Mr David Lewis a very goodnatured, good-
looking old gentleman whas [for who] has been very kind to Tom
and George and me. As for those fellows the Brickmakers they are
always passing to and fro. I mus'n't forget the two old maiden
Ladies in well walk who have a Lap dog between them, that they
25   are very anxious about. It is a corpulent Little Beast whom it is
necessary to coax along with an ivory-tipp'd cane. Carlo our
Neighbour Mrs Brawne's dog and it meet sometimes. Lappy
thinks Carlo a devil of a fellow and so do his Mistresses. Well they
may—he would sweep 'em all down at a run; all for the Joke of it.
30   I shall desire him to pursue the fable of the Boys and the frogs:
though he prefers the tongues and the Bones. You shall hear from
me again the day after tomorrow—

Your affectionate Brother
John Keats

15   *the heath* – Hampstead Heath was clearly visible from the house at that
time.

To Fanny Brawne, June 1820

Keats had spent May separated from Fanny, living in another part of London.
In this letter his jealousy is voiced.

To FANNY BRAWNE
Wednesday [June 1820]

Wednesday Morng.

My dearest Girl,

I have been a walk this morning with a book in my hand, but as
usual I have been occupied with nothing but you: I wish I could
5   say in an agreeable manner. I am tormented day and night. They
talk of my going to Italy. 'Tis certain I shall never recover if I am to
be so long separate from you; yet with all this devotion to you I
cannot persuade myself into any confidence of you. Past experience connected with the fact of my long separation from you gives
10 me agonies which are scarcely to be talked of. When your mother
comes I shall be very sudden and expert in asking her whether you
have been to Mrs Dilke's, for she might say no to make me easy. I
am literally worn to death, which seems my only recourse. I cannot
forget what has pass'd. What? nothing with a man of the world,
15 but to me deathful. I will get rid of this as much as possible. When
you were in the habit of flirting with Brown you would have left
off, could your own heart have felt one half of one pang mine did.
Brown is a good sort of Man—he did not know he was doing me
to death by inches. I feel the effect of every one of those hours in
20 my side now; and for that cause, though he has done me many
services, though I know his love and friendship for me, though at
this moment I should be without pence were it not for his assis-
tance, I will never see or speak to him until we are both old men, if
we are to be. I *will* resent my heart having been made a football.
25 You will call this madness. I have heard you say that it was not
unpleasant to wait a few years—you have amusements—your
mind is away—you have not brooded over one idea as I have, and
how should you? You are to me an object intensely desireable—the
air I breathe in a room empty of you is unhealthy. I am not the same
30 to you—no—you can wait—you have a thousand activities—you
can be happy without me. Any party, any thing to fill up the day
has been enough. How have you pass'd this month? Who have you
smil'd with? All this may seem savage in me. You do not feel as I
do—you do not know what it is to love—one day you may—your
35 time is not come. Ask yourself how many unhappy hours Keats
has caused you in Loneliness. For myself I have been a Martyr the

whole time, and for this reason I speak; the confession is forc'd
from me by the torture. I appeal to you by the blood of that Christ
you believe in: Do not write to me if you have done anything this
40 month which it would have pained me to have seen. You may have
altered—if you have not—if you still behave in dancing rooms and
other societies as I have seen you—I do not want to live—if you
have done so I wish this coming night may be my last. I cannot live
without, and not only you but *chaste you; virtuous you.* The Sun rises
45 and sets, the day passes, and you follow the bent of your inclina-
tion to a certain extent—you have no conception of the quantity of
miserable feeling that passes through me in a day.—Be serious!
Love is not a plaything—and again do not write unless you can do
it with a crystal conscience. I would sooner die for want of you
50 than—

> Yours for ever
> J. Keats

To CHARLES BROWN
Thursday 30 Nov. 1820

Rome. 30 November 1820.

My dear Brown,

'Tis the most difficult thing in the world to me to write a letter.
My stomach continues so bad, that I feel it worse on opening any
book,—yet I am much better than I was in Quarantine. Then I am
5   afraid to encounter the proing and conning of any thing interesting
to me in England. I have an habitual feeling of my real life having
past, and that I am leading a posthumous existence. God knows
how it would have been—but it appears to me—however, I will
not speak of that subject. I must have been at Bedhampton nearly

To Charles Brown, 30 November 1820

Keats was in Rome at the time of writing this letter. He had travelled there,
with his friend Joseph Severn, for the sake of his health.

19 *walking with her* – a reference to Fanny Brawne.

28 **** – These asterisks represent friends' names which were omitted by
Brown when he made a copy of this letter.

10   at the time you were writing to me from Chichester—how unfor-
     tunate—and to pass on the river too! There was my star pre-domi-
     nant! I cannot answer any thing in your letter, which followed me
     from Naples to Rome, because I am afraid to look it over again. I
     am so weak (in mind) that I cannot bear the sight of any hand
15   writing of a friend I love so much as I do you. Yet I ride the little
     horse,—and, at my worst, even in Quarantine, summoned up
     more puns, in a sort of desperation, in one week than in any year
     of my life. There is one thought enough to kill me—I have been
     well, healthy, alert &c, walking with her—and now—the knowl-
20   edge of contrast, feeling for light and shade, all that information
     (primitive sense) necessary for a poem are great enemies to the
     recovery of the stomach. There, you rogue, I put you to the tor-
     ture,—but you must bring your philosophy to bear—as I do mine,
     really—or how should I be able to live? Dr. Clarke is very attentive
25   to me; he says, there is very little the matter with my lungs, but my
     stomach, he says, is very bad. I am well disappointed in hearing
     good news from George,—for it runs in my head we shall all die
     young. I have not written to ***** yet, which he must think very
     neglectful; being anxious to send him a good account of my health,
30   I have delayed it from week to week. If I recover, I will do all in my
     power to correct the mistakes made during sickness; and if I should
     not, all my faults will be forgiven. I shall write to *** to-morrow, or
     next day. I will write to ***** in the middle of next week. Severn is
     very well, though he leads so dull a life with me. Remember me to
35   all friends, and tell **** I should not have left London without
     taking leave of him, but from being so low in body and mind. Write
     to George as soon as you receive this, and tell him how I am, as far
     as you can guess;—and also a note to my sister—who walks about
     my imagination like a ghost—she is so like Tom. I can scarcely bid
40   you good bye even in a letter. I always made an awkward bow.

                                         God bless you!
                                              John Keats

CRITICAL APPROACHES

During his lifetime Keats's poetry was the subject of much controversy. His friends declared that he was a genius; his friends' political enemies thought him foolish.

In **Critical Approaches** you will read about the background to the period in which Keats was writing as well as different reactions to his poetry from the nineteenth century to the present day. Such details, together with the **Activities** which follow will help you to understand aspects of Keats's poetry more fully.

Keats's Life

John Keats was born in London in 1795. His parents managed the Swan and Hoop Inn where John and his younger brothers, George, Tom and his sister Frances (Fanny) lived. The death of their father in a riding accident in 1804 was followed by their mother's second marriage; the children moved to live with their grandparents that same year. Their mother returned to join the family in 1810 but died of tuberculosis soon after.

Guardians were appointed to look after the financial interests of the Keats children, but, unfortunately, although there was ample money in the fund, financial concerns were a worry to the children throughout their lives. This was partly because the details of their grandfather's will were unclear and led to legal disputes within the family.

Keats attended a small private school in Enfield, north London. Here, within a civilized atmosphere (there was no caning), he met his life-long friend, Charles Cowden Clarke, the headmaster's son. After leaving the school in 1810 he became an apothecary's apprentice, learning to prepare ointments, medicines and pills. At this stage he was also an earnest reader: during many of his frequent meetings with Charles Cowden Clarke, literature was the subject of discussion. In 1815 he enrolled at Guy's Hospital where he attended lectures, worked in wards and watched surgeons perform operations on conscious patients (anaesthetics had not yet been developed) in conditions that would shock us today. In 1816 he qualified in his profession when he passed the newly established examination which had been introduced to raise the status of apothecaries, and, in that same year, Keats informed his guardian of a major decision: he planned to be a poet rather than an apothecary.

At that stage in his life Keats was meeting regularly with figures who were well known in artistic circles. Key figures include Leigh Hunt (editor of *The Examiner*, a weekly newspaper that supported reform), Joseph Severn (a painter) and Benjamin Haydon (an artist who produced huge paintings on epic themes, and included Keats's portrait in his painting *Christ's Entry into Jerusalem*). Keats was also acquainted with Wordsworth, Coleridge, Shelley, Hazlitt, Lamb and Godwin. Many of these figures are mentioned in Keats's letters which supply us with a rich source of biography as well as an insight into Keats's ideas about writing poetry.

In 1818, the same year as his brother George married and left for America, Keats's other brother, Tom, died of tuberculosis. This was also the year that Keats met Fanny Brawne. Fanny, with her sister, brother and widowed mother, rented half of a property in Wentworth Place in Hampstead that belonged to Keats's friends, Charles Brown and Charles Dilke. After Tom's death, Keats moved in with Brown at Wentworth Place, and in October 1819, he became engaged to Fanny. At that stage Keats was increasingly unwell; he also had pressing financial worries. In 1820, after two lung haemorrhages, Keats accepted his doctor's advice and planned to travel to Italy as a way of surviving the winter. He set sail with his friend Joseph Severn in September of that year, and died in Rome a few months later, on 23 February 1821.

The time-chart which follows offers a skeleton of events in Keats's life listed against what was happening in British and European history.

Responses from Keats's Contemporaries

There is no doubt from the early reviews that Keats's poetry was considered by some to be disturbing because of the vocabulary and versification which were so different from the prevailing literary taste. A reading of a selection of Alexander Pope's poems (extracts from *The Rape of the Lock* or *The Dunciad* for example), with their preponderance of end-stopped rhyming couplets and satirical tone, will illustrate clearly some of these differences.

But criticism of Keats's work was also a political issue because he was seen as a young poet who was voicing a protest against the established

Time Chart

	Events in Keats's life		Other Events
1795	Birth of John Keats in London (31 October)		
1797	Birth of George (brother)		
		1798	Wordsworth & Coleridge: *Lyrical Ballads*
1799	Birth of Tom (brother)		
1801	Birth of Edward (brother)		
1802	Edward dies Starts attending a boarding school in Enfield, north London	1802	Temporary peace with France
1803	Birth of Frances (Fanny: sister)		
1804	Father dies His mother remarries Children move to their grandparents' home		
1805	Grandfather dies	1805	Battle of Trafalgar
		1809	*Quarterly* founded Birth of Darwin Birth of Tennyson
1810	Mother dies of tuberculosis Leaves school to become apothecary's apprentice		
		1812	Birth of Charles Dickens
1814	Grandmother dies		
1815	Enters Guy's Hospital as a student	1815	Battle of Waterloo End of Napoleonic Wars
1816	Qualifies as an apothecary but decides to be a poet		
1817	Moves to Hampstead *Poems* published	1817	Jane Austen dies
1818	*Endymion* published Meets Fanny Brawne Brother Tom dies Moves to Wentworth Place, Hampstead	1818	*Blackwood's* attacks Keats as a member of the 'Cockney School of Poetry'
1819	Writes the major odes Becomes engaged to Fanny Brawne	1819	Byron: *Don Juan* Cantos I and II
1820	Severe lung haemorrhage *Lamia* volume appears Leaves for Italy with Severn	1820	Prince Regent becomes George IV
1821	Dies of tuberculosis (23 February)	1821	Shelley: *Adonais*

order of his day. It was a time of deep political and social divisions, created by the Napoleonic Wars (1807–15), and of political censorship of newspapers and literature. Indeed, in 1809 the Tory establishment founded *The Quarterly*, an influential literary magazine which had the power to dictate the reputation and sales of the publications it reviewed. Keats and his writings were attacked viciously by this magazine and by *Blackwood's* and *The British Critic*. To reviewers in these magazines, Keats, who had no university or classical education, was a social upstart for presuming to write poetry at all.

Keats was 21 when his first collection of poems appeared in 1817. The volume presents many different kinds of writing: narrative (*I stood tiptoe upon a little hill*); sonnets (*On First Looking into Chapman's Homer* and *On the Sea*, for example); and verse epistles addressed to family and friends. The collection was dedicated to Leigh Hunt, an influential literary figure of the day. (See page 275 for more details of Leigh Hunt and other contemporaries.)

Reviews were sparse and disappointment led Keats to try a new publisher for his next collection, *Endymion* (1818), in which he used Greek mythology to create a pastoral narrative. In referring to the Greek stories of classical gods here and in later poems (*Hyperion* and *The Fall of Hyperion*, for example), Keats was following a fashion of his time. He had no knowledge of Greek and, therefore, read guides to mythology in order to provide the background he needed for his poems.

Critical responses to *Endymion* were split dramatically. The favourable pieces were, however, outweighed by unsigned attacks in *The Quarterly* and *Blackwood's* which were dismissive of Keats's links with Leigh Hunt and his literary circle as well as their political views. Keats was associated with the so-called 'Cockney' school of poetry, and at that time Cockney referred not only to a native Londoner but also had derogatory overtones which implied affectation and vulgar behaviour.

Reactions to Keats's third volume in 1820 (which includes *Lamia, Isabella, The Eve of St Agnes, Hyperion* and many of his odes) were once again split. Keats had his supporters – Wordsworth, for example, expressed his admiration – but the critical attacks were influential and Keats's reputation took time to recover. Indeed, a summary of the situation up to 1848, over thirty years after Keats's first publication, is neatly given in a review from the *New Monthly Magazine* (September 1848):

It was the misfortune of Keats as a poet, to be either extravagantly praised or unmercifully condemned. The former had its origins in the generous partialities of friendship, somewhat obtrusively displayed; the latter in some degree, to resentment of that friendship, connected as it was with party politics, and peculiar views of society as well as of poetry.

Later Reaction

In 1848 the publication of Richard Monckton Milnes's *Life, Letters, and Literary Remains, of John Keats,* featuring unpublished poems, letters and reminiscences supplied by friends, brought Keats some of the fame he deserved.

During the middle of the nineteenth century Keats's reputation was furthered by the paintings of Dante Gabriel Rossetti, Holman Hunt and other painter-poets associated with the Pre-Raphaelites. These painters were attracted by the medieval world of many of Keats's poems – a world viewed as remote from practical life – and as a result scenes from Keats's *Eve of St Agnes* and *La Belle Dame sans Merci* were exhibited in galleries.

Another important consideration in the development of Keats's reputation was the appearance of some of his poems in Palgrave's influential *Golden Treasury* (1861). But a blow followed a few years later when, in 1878, the publication of his letters to Fanny Brawne caused embarrassment in literary circles.

However, in 1880 a major book-length study of Keats (written by Mrs F. W. Owen) was published, and by the end of that century Keats's poetry had been written about approvingly by G. M. Hopkins, Matthew Arnold, Swinburne and Robert Bridges; his reputation as one of the major English poets was securely established.

During the twentieth century a large number of critical publications have given attention to many different aspects of Keats's writing. Keats's reputation has also been helped by the appearance of some very detailed and accessible biographies by, for example, Robert Gittings and Stephen Coote. (See the bibliography on page 295 for further details.)

Keats's letters, which contain much evidence of this writer as a thinker, have also served to heighten his reputation in recent years. Indeed, his appeal continues as can be seen, for example, through the pages of the established *Keats-Shelley Review* (formerly *The Keats-*

Shelley Memorial Bulletin). Keats enthusiasts are also welcome at the house in Hampstead where Keats lived from 1818. Visitors can wander through the restored rooms and make use of the Keats Memorial Library that holds a substantial stock of relevant material. The house in Rome in which Keats died, 26 Piazza di Spagna, alongside the Spanish steps, is also open to the public. It is now the Keats/Shelley Memorial House.

Approaches to the Odes

You might find it helpful to find and compare definitions of an ode as found in different books of reference. Some may remind you that, in ancient literature, an ode was a poem intended, or adapted, to be sung; others may refer to the term's modern use as a lyric, dignified in subject, feeling and in style, as well as complexly organized in form.

In order to explore the way Keats develops the ode it is helpful to know of the tradition of celebratory odes which extends from Pindar, who lived in Greece in the sixth century BC. His poems were usually organized into three stanzas of which the third was of a different form from the rest. Elements of this form of ode, as well as odes which explore abstract ideas, are found in English poets from the seventeenth century onwards. Indeed, Wordsworth's *Ode: Intimations of Immortality* and Coleridge's *Dejection* are well-known contemporary examples.

Five of the poems that are central to this discussion (*Ode to Psyche, Ode on Indolence, Ode to a Nightingale, Ode on a Grecian Urn* and *Ode on Melancholy,* all written in the spring/summer of 1819) feature the word ode in their title, and to this group is usually added *To Autumn*. It is well worth re-reading these poems as a group and considering ways in which they are linked in form and subject. Details outlined in **Activities** which follows will help you to bring the relevant ideas together.

Many have commented on the way in which the style and moods of Keats's odes appear to have grown out of his experience with the sonnet form. *On First Looking into Chapman's Homer* and *When I have fears* are two of many instances where Keats works within the fourteen-line framework and rhyming scheme of a sonnet. The structure of *On First Looking into Chapman's Homer* divides into two parts: an eight-line section (octave) followed by a six-line section (sestet) adopting the pattern of a Petrarchan sonnet; in *When I have fears,* three four-line sections (quatrains) are followed by a closing rhyming couplet adopting the pattern of a Shakespearean sonnet.

Four of the group of odes noted above use ten-line stanzas which incorporate features of the sonnet (quatrain and sestet); *To Autumn* with its eleven-line pattern establishes similar links. *Ode to Psyche*, however, has stanzas of different lengths – but the sonnet features are still in evidence despite the introduction of lines with three stresses (instead of the usual five) and the fact that some lines are left unrhymed. After the irregular structure of *Ode to Psyche,* the other odes appear much tighter in form, although each has interesting variations. Thus within the odes Keats was introducing innovation in form while at the same time writing poems of a length that allowed for careful development of thought and feeling.

Over the years there has been much discussion as to which of Keats's odes is the most successful. T. S. Eliot thought *Ode to Psyche* the finest, whereas Kenneth Allott called it the Cinderella of the group. The qualities of *To Autumn* have been praised by many; *Ode on Indolence* has been dismissed by some as a failure. It is well worth taking your time when discussing Keats's odes in order to decide on your own response to each of these remarkable poems which face and explore time, death and suffering while, at the same time, presenting a belief in the sustaining power of the human imagination.

The Letters

Keats wrote many letters to family and friends which provide a detailed account of his life, his writings and his ideas on poetry. It seems that the special qualities of the letters were recognized by those who received them; the letters were copied and quoted by his friends.

In the selection of letters printed in this publication (arranged chronologically alongside the poems), you will find some direct links with the poems; for example, the extract from the letter of 21 September 1819 describes the background to *To Autumn*, and the comments on the vale of soul-making (21 April 1819) anticipate the odes. You will also find detailed exploration of ideas about the composition of poetry as given in the famous discussion of 'Negative Capability' (21 December 1817) that Keats saw as essential to great poetry. You will, in addition, find in the letters an extraordinary record of Keats's life, concerns and development as a poet.

EXPLORATIONS AND ESSAYS

Activities

The activities and tasks in this section are designed to explore in detail specific aspects of selected poems. They should be regarded as a springboard to discussion, research, evaluation, personal response and writing. Most can be done individually or tackled as group work.

On First Looking into Chapman's Homer

1 In the opening lines of this Petrarchan sonnet (see **Critical Approaches,** page 279), Keats introduces a metaphor to describe his experience of reading various poets. What key phrases would you select to illustrate the effectiveness of this metaphor?

2 What does the simile introduced in line 9 reveal about the emotions of the speaker?

3 Patterns of alliteration appear in the final lines of this sonnet; the repetition of the 's', for example. What effect does the use of alliteration have on the pace of your reading of the final lines of the poem?

Endymion

1 It has been argued that lines 232–306 (divided into five roughly equal sections) share characteristics with Keats's later odes. Which of the odes seems to you to offer the most obvious points of comparison? You might find it helpful to present your arguments in the form of a chart which brings attention to the shared features.

2 What argument is being presented in lines 824–42? Examine these lines closely and then give your reaction to the view presented.

3 Explore the extended simile in lines 828–31. What effect does Keats achieve by including this simile?

4 John Barnard, in his study of Keats, says of this poem 'Endymion's plot is an argument for the essential interconnectedness of human love and the truth of ideal beauty'. How far would you agree with this point of view? Support your response with close textual reference.

On sitting down to read King Lear once again

This sonnet is inspired by Shakespeare, both in subject and in form. It is the first sonnet by Keats to adopt a closing couplet following the established Shakespearean form of the sonnet. Examine closely the structure of this sonnet, paying particular attention to the way in which Keats develops his argument within the given form. (**Critical Approaches** pages 279–80 may be helpful here.)

When I have fears

1 Examine closely the Shakespearean sonnet form used and, as you do so, summarize the points made in each of the quatrains. (**Critical Approaches** pages 279 may be helpful here.)

2 What does Keats acknowledge in the closing couplet of this poem as being capable of pushing all personal concerns out of his head?

Lines on the Mermaid Tavern

Note, with examples, how Keats succeeds here in establishing a humorous approach to his subject.

Isabella

1 What effect is achieved by the repetition of 'Why were they proud?' in stanza XVI?

2 Consider the poet's address to Boccaccio, in which he asks for forgiveness, in lines 145–60. What do these lines add to the poem?

3 What point of comparison is being made between the ghost of a murdered man and blood-hounds in lines 219–21?

4 Select the words and phrases you would choose to illustrate the way in which Keats creates atmosphere in this poem.

5 From the extract you have read, what do you consider to be the central theme(s) of *Isabella*?

Hyperion

Book I

1 In the opening description of Saturn and his wife Thea, Keats emphasizes the size and desolation of the two figures. Select words and phrases that strengthen these aspects.

2 Identify the words and phrases that succeed in capturing the essence of Hyperion from his introduction, beginning on line 164.

3 Lines 251–304 describe the battle between Hyperion's light and the conquering dark. Examine these lines closely, noting the images used and the effects achieved.

Book II

1 Outline your impression of the place where the fallen Titans have congregated. How do the descriptions of individual Titans add to the picture?

2 Read carefully the account of the debate started by Saturn (line 110) with contributions from Oceanus (172ff), Clymene (248ff) and Enceladus (309ff). Which lines do you consider central to the argument that each presents?

3 Explain what details of Hyperion's entrance (346ff) make it plain that he has accepted defeat.

Book III

1 Some have argued that the poetry in Book III is less magnificent and less clear in meaning than the language of Books I and II. Do you agree? Identify the phrases you could use to support your view.

2 Look closely at the way that both Mnemosyne and Apollo are presented in this book. Note down the words and phrases that you consider to be the most memorable in the presentation of each.

The Eve of St. Agnes

1 We are presented here with a love story in which the young lovers attempt to overcome obstacles. Make a list of some of the obstacles that feature in the poem.

2 This poem is written in stanzas which follow the pattern that was developed by Edmund Spenser for *The Faerie Queene*. Each stanza consists of nine lines (eight of iambic pentameters and the ninth extended to a twelve-syllable iambic line) with a tight rhyming scheme. What effect is achieved by the lengthened final line in each stanza?

3 Some critics have commented that the reference to a limping hare in the opening stanza prepares us for our introduction to the vulnerable Madeline later in the poem. What other links can be made between the

atmosphere established in the opening stanzas of the poem and the world that Madeline inhabits?

4   Details of Porphyro's plan are given in stanza XIX. What disturbing details are noted here and how do they affect your attitude towards the plan?

5   Stanza XXX brings out a clear contrast between Madeline and Porphyro. She is presented as clean and pure, sleeping in 'smooth', 'lavender'd' sheets; he is associated with exotic, sticky sweets. What other images within the poem bring out the contrast between the two?

6   In September 1819, Keats suggested alterations to this poem, including a rewrite of stanza XXXVI and the two preceding lines:

> See, while she speaks his arms encroaching slow,
> Have zoned her, heart to heart, – loud, loud the dark winds blow!
>
> ### XXXVI
>
> For on the midnight came a tempest fell;
> More sooth, for that his quick rejoinder flows
> Into her burning ear; and still the spell
> Unbroken guards her in serene repose.
> With her wild dream he mingled, as a rose
> Marrieth its odour to a violet.
> Still, still she dreams, louder the frost wind blows.

This was, however, rejected by his publisher on the grounds that the changes made the poem too sexually explicit. Some have argued that one of the strengths of stanza XXXVI as printed – in which Porphyro becomes part of Madeline's dream and fulfils it – is that it can be read innocently. What is your view of the two versions of stanza XXXVI? Explain which you think to be the better and why.

7   Underline some of the unsettling details that appear in the three final stanzas of this poem. Then discuss ways in which these details could be seen to be an appropriate close to the poem.

8   This poem has been described as 'the most cinematic of Keats's poems'. What do you understand by this statement? Discuss with a partner or group whether you think this is a helpful comment on *The Eve of St. Agnes*. A focus on pace and contrasts could provide a useful starting-point to your discussion.

La Belle Dame sans Merci

1 In this poem Keats uses a variation of the ballad form. Brainstorm any modern or older associations connected with the ballad, and then list features of the ballad form.

2 It is usual for each stanza in a ballad to follow the following pattern of stresses per line: 4, 3, 4, 3. Keats chooses to make each fourth line in his poem shorter – 2 stresses rather than 4. Read the poem aloud and decide what effect this shortened line gives.

3 Make a list of the words and phrases Keats uses to create the medieval atmosphere of the poem.

4 This poem. following the tradition of a ballad, includes much repetition. There are, however, some subtle changes within the repeated lines, e.g. 'The sedge has withered' becomes 'The sedge is withered'. Examine such changes carefully and decide how each affects your reading of the poem.

5 'Whether La Belle Dame's love for the knight was feigned or true, or whether his dream was true, we cannot tell. Nor do we know whether he chooses to loiter by the withering, birdless lake, or whether his dream experience ties him there against his wish.' (Walter Jackson Bate) Bearing this comment in mind, what would you say about the world inhabited by the knight, and what do you think is going to happen to him?

Ode to Psyche

1 What effect does Keats achieve by referring to aspects of Greek worship using repeated negatives in stanza 2?

2 This ode appears irregular on the page, but as you explore it closely you will discover details of content as well as structure that hold the unequal stanzas together. What is the dominant rhythmic pattern within the poem? What links can you find between the rhyming patterns in this poem and what you would expect to find in a sonnet which follows the Shakespearean or Petrarchan form? (see **Critical Approaches,** pages 279–80.)

3 In the final section of the poem (50–67) Keats outlines how he can worship Psyche 'in some untrodden region of my mind'. Explore the way in which he develops this central image in the final stanza.

Ode on Indolence

1 The epigraph is a quotation from St Matthew's Gospel (chapter 6, verse 28) in which Jesus describes the lilies of the field: 'And why take ye thought for raiment? Consider the lilies of the field, how they grow; they toil not, neither do they spin'. What in your view is the relevance of this epigraph to the poem which follows?

2 Discuss Keats's reaction to the three mysterious figures. In what way does that reaction seem appropriate to the title of the poem?

3 What lines would you select as illustration of a satirical tone within this poem? It has been argued that *Ode on Indolence* is less successful than many of Keats's other poems because the satirical tone of some of the lines jars with the remainder of the poem. Do you agree with this view?

Ode to a Nightingale

1 Stanza 4 opens with a note of dismissal. Read the opening three stanzas closely and then decide what the poet is dismissing here.

2 Explore the way in which Keats evokes all the senses in stanza 5.

3 Describe in your own words the poet's attitude to death in stanza 6.

4 What point about the bird does Keats make in the historical review outlined in stanza 7?

5 What are the various abilities attributed to the bird throughout the poem, and how do they relate to the poem's theme?

6 Commenting on the last two lines of the poem, John Barnard writes 'Keats yearns to attain the pure being of the natural world, in which the nightingale's "full-throated ease" appears a perfect equivalent for human song (lyric poetry)'. What do you take to be the differences and similarities between the bird's song and the act of writing poetry?

7 Notice that in this ode Keats has introduced a short eighth line (three stresses only) in each stanza, a pattern which is not followed in later odes. Look closely at the structure of each stanza in this poem and in *Ode on a Grecian Urn* which follows. Make a note of similarities and differences, and then discuss your findings with a partner. In your discussion, focus particularly on any points that do not appear on both your lists.

Ode on a Grecian Urn

1 Three scenes depicted on the urn are outlined in this ode. Select details of each and discuss how these scenes are related to the themes that Keats explores in this poem.

2 In what way do the details noted in stanza 4 reveal to the reader the speaker's involvement in the world pictured on the urn?

3 It has been suggested that the fifth stanza 'does not read as smoothly as the others'. What evidence do you find to support this view?

4 Critics have suggested that some of the issues raised in this poem are also faced in *Ode to a Nightingale*. After you have read both poems, discuss with a partner what you think is meant by this and how far you agree.

5 There is no 'I' in this ode. How does this affect your reading of it, by comparison with, for example, *Ode on Indolence* or *Ode to a Nightingale*?

6 The final lines of this ode (49–50) have evoked much discussion. It has been argued, for example, that these lines are meaningless and thus a blemish on the poem; they have also been viewed as philosophically interesting but, nevertheless, an inappropriate conclusion to the ode. Do you agree with either of these positions? What links if any can you see between these final lines and the previous stanzas of the poem?

Ode on Melancholy

1 What advice is given in the first and second stanzas about ways to avoid giving way to melancholy?

2 Examine closely the references to eating and drinking in stanzas 2 and 3. What aspects of appetite make such references relevant within the context of the poem?

3 How does Keats succeed in presenting Melancholy as a god-like being in this poem?

4 There has been much discussion of the ambiguity of the closing lines of this poem. For example, do you understand 'Can burst Joy's grape' to mean 'is capable of experiencing joy to the full' or 'is capable of seeing through joy and understanding it for what it really is'? Discuss the closing lines in detail and then decide which reading you support and why.

Lamia

Part I

1 It has been argued that lines 1–45 establish the poem's main themes of passion and sexual love. What evidence can you find to support this view?

2 Examine closely the initial description of Lamia (47–67) and the section which describes her transformation (146–170). Select key words and phrases from these passages and indicate their effectiveness within the poem as a whole.

3 Here, as in *Endymion*, Keats uses heroic couplets. Find examples of ways in which he achieves variation within the lines of this poem. You may wish to consider the use of punctuation (line 151), the introduction of extended lines (line 91) and the appearance of rhyming triplets (lines 61–63).

Part II

4 In what ways do the opening lines (1–15) contribute to the poem as a whole?

5 In Part II Keats records the changing relationship of Lycius and Lamia. Indicate which words and phrases bring attention to the way that Lycius begins to exert his will and Lamia's reactions to this change.

6 Heroic couplets, partly because of their use by Alexander Pope (see **Critical Approaches,** page 275), are often associated with satire. Are there occasions within *Lamia* – the narrator's asides to the reader, for example – where you can find evidence of Keats exploring the humorous quality of the rhyme?

To Autumn

1 Discuss with a partner what you consider to be the main theme (or themes) of this poem.

2 Study closely the four personifications of autumn introduced in stanza 2. How does each explore the theme(s) of the poem?

3 Notice the way in which the verbs in stanza 1 suggest activity. How would you describe the change of mood of stanza 2? What features of the language contribute to this change?

4 What ideas are introduced into stanza 3? How do these ideas link with the rest of the poem?

5 It has been argued that the attraction of *To Autumn* lies partly in its celebration of the ideal relationship between man and nature. How far do you agree with this view?

The Fall of Hyperion

1 The sub-title 'a Dream' appears at the start of this poem, although the dream itself does not begin until line 19. Prepare your own summary of the arguments put forward in the opening 18 lines.

2 The discussion between the narrator and Moneta in lines 136–215 focuses on the poet's role within the world. What evidence can you find there for the presentation of the poet as an active rather than a reclusive figure?

3 What impression do you get of the priestess Moneta from the way she is described in lines 256–58 and 260–61, and the arguments she puts forward? What is her role within the poem? Compare the presentation of Moneta with the figure of Mnemosyne as presented in *Hyperion*.

4 Consider the links between *Hyperion* and *The Fall of Hyperion*. What evidence is there that *The Fall of Hyperion* acts as a prologue to *Hyperion?*

Essays

- Keats has been called a poet of touch and taste. Explore this idea in detail through close discussion of a selection of relevant poems.

- Discuss Keats's use of classical mythology in his poetry, making particular reference to extracts from *Endymion* and one other poem of your choice.

- Write a critical appreciation of *La Belle Dame sans Merci*. Discuss briefly how typical this poem is of Keats's work.

- Through close discussion of two or three sonnets by Keats, consider this poet's skill as a writer of sonnets.

- Look again at the opening three stanzas of *The Eve of St. Agnes*. How far do these lines prepare us for what is to follow?

- By close examination of two or three poems of your choice, explore Keats's use of imagery and the effects achieved.

- In what ways has your reading of a selection of Keats's letters affected your understanding of and response to his poems?

- Explore the ways in which Keats creates a medieval world through close discussion of two poems of your choice.

- To what extent do you accept the view that Keats's odes are variations on a series of central ideas? Be ready to support your argument by close discussion of at least two odes.

- Choose a theme that interests you in Keats's poetry. Explore how Keats presents that theme in two or three poems of your choice.

WRITING AN ESSAY
ABOUT POETRY

Your own personal response to a poet and his or her work is of major importance when writing an essay on poetry, either as part of your course or as an examination question. However, this personal response needs to be based on a solid concept of how poetry works, so you must clearly show that you understand the methods the poet uses to convey the message and ideas of the poem to the reader. In most cases, unless it is relevant to your answer, you should not pad out your essay with biographical or background material.

Planning

Look carefully at the wording of the question. Underline the important words and ideas. Make sure you apply your mind to these key elements of the question and then explore them in the essay.

Bring all your knowledge of, and opinions on, a poet and his or her poetry to this first stage of writing. Brainstorm your ideas and always combine these thoughts in a plan that shows the development and intention of your answer. Your plan must outline the structure of your essay. In exam conditions, the plan and the direction of your comments may take you only a few minutes and should be little more than a way of laying out your ideas in order. However the plan must be an outline of how and where you are going to link your evidence to the opinions and concepts of the essay. Reject any ideas which are not relevant at the planning stage. Remember that your plan should be arranged around your ideas and not the chronological order of a poem or a poet's work, or your essay will be weakened.

Writing

Your introduction must implicitly or, if you wish, explicitly make the teacher or examiner realize that you understand the question.

Don't spend a lot of time spotting, defining and examining poetic techniques and form. If you do identify these features, then you must be sure of the poetic terms and be able to show why they are significant in the verse and to the poet's attempts to create a 'meaning' and a message.

Make absolutely sure that your answer is clear and that it tackles the issues in the question precisely. Try to offer points for discussion and apply your knowledge in an interesting way. Don't go ahead and disregard what the question asks you to write about, then write the essay you want to write. Don't waffle, don't write too elaborately or use terms vaguely; at the same time, don't be too heavy-handed with your views. Strive to put your opinions directly and accurately.

In exam conditions be aware of the time, and if you are running out of your allotted span then make sure that you put down your most important ideas in the minutes left. Try to leave a few minutes to revise and proof-read your script. Be sure that the points you have made make sense and are well supported by evidence. Don't try to introduce new ideas as you write unless they are essential to your essay. Often these extra thoughts can distract you from the logic of your argument. If it is essential, then refer back to your plan and slot the idea into the right part of the essay.

Bring your ideas together at the end of the essay. Make sure that you have put your views clearly and, if necessary, express the main thrust of your views or argument again.

Quotations

Quotations are a vital source of evidence for the viewpoints and ideas you express in your essay. Try not to misquote and remember that when using extracts of more than a few words you should place them separately outside your text as they would be laid out in the poem.

If you follow the advice here you will produce a clear, relevant and logical essay. Try to spend time reading and listening to the comments of your teacher and make your own notes on your work for revision purposes.

Andrew Whittle

A NOTE FROM A CHIEF EXAMINER

Your examination script is the medium through which you communicate with your examiner. As a student, you will have studied what writers say and how they say it; your examiner will assess what *you* say and how you say it. This is the simple process through which your knowledge and understanding of the texts you have studied is converted into your examination result.

The questions which you will find on your examination paper have been designed to enable you to display your ability to engage in short, highly concentrated explorations of particular aspects of the texts which you have studied. There is no intention to trick you into making mistakes, rather to enable you to demonstrate to your examiner your knowledge and understanding. Questions take a variety of forms. For a poetry text, you may be asked to concentrate on one poem, or a particular group of them, and provide detailed examination of some features of the writing. You may be asked to range widely throughout a poet's work, exploring specified aspects of his or her style and themes. You may be asked to provide a considered personal reaction to a critical evaluation of the poet's work.

Whatever the question, you are, ultimately, being asked to explore what and how, content and style. Equally, you are being asked for a personal response. You are communicating to your examiner your own understanding of the text, and your reactions to it, based on the studies you have undertaken.

All of this may seem very simple, if not self-evident, but it is worthwhile to devote some time to thinking about what an examination is, and how it works. By doing so, you will understand why it is so important that you should prepare yourself for your examination in two principal ways: first, by thorough, thoughtful and analytical textual study, making your own well-informed evaluation of the work of a particular writer, considering what he or she is conveying to you, how this is done, how you react, and what has made you respond in that way; then, by practising the writing skills which you will need to convey all these things to your examiner.

When assessing your script and awarding marks, examiners are working to guidelines which instruct them to look for a variety of different qualities in an essay.

These are some of the things which an examiner will consider.

- How well has the candidate understood the essay question and the given task? Is the argument, and the material used to support it, entirely relevant?

- Is quotation used aptly, and textual reference employed skillfully in discussion?

- Is the candidate aware of how and why the writer has crafted material in a particular way?

- Is there evidence of engagement with the text, close analytical reading, and awareness of subtleties in interpretation?

- Does the candidate have the necessary vocabulary, both general and critical, to express his or her understanding lucidly? Are technical terms integrated into discussion?

- Can the candidate provide an interesting, clearly expressed and structured line of argument, which fully displays a well-informed personal response?

From these points, you should be able to see the kind of approach to examination questions which you should avoid. Re-hashed notes, second-hand opinion, unsupported assertion and arid copies of marginal jottings have no place in a good script. Don't fall into the trap of reproducing a pre-planned essay. Undoubtedly you will find (if your preparation has been thorough) that you are drawing on ideas which you have already explored in other essays, but all material used must be properly adapted to the task you are given. Don't take a narrative approach; paraphrase cannot replace analysis. Do not, under any circumstances, copy out chunks of introduction or critical notes from your text in an open book examination. Nor do you need to quote at excessive length; your examiner knows the text.

It is inevitable that, when writing in examination conditions, you will only use quite a small amount of the material you have studied in order to answer a particular question. Don't feel that what you are not using has been wasted. It hasn't. All your studies will have informed the understanding you display in a succinct, well-focused answer, and will equip you to write a good essay.

Virginia Graham
Chief Examiner for A level English Literature

SELECT BIBLIOGRAPHY

The details which follow are selected from a wide range of publications including editions of Keats's own writings, biographies and critical responses.

Keats's Writings

Elizabeth Cook (ed.), *John Keats* (Oxford University Press: The Oxford Authors, 1990) provides a one-volume edition of Keats's writings which includes almost all his poetry, about one-third of his surviving letters plus some additional prose. It also features some useful notes and a glossary of classical names.

Robert Gittings (ed.) *Letters of John Keats: a new selection* (Oxford University Press, 1970, rev.ed. 1975) is a useful edition with helpful notes.

Biography

Robert Gittings, *John Keats* (Heinemann, 1968: Penguin, 1971) provides a comprehensive account of Keats's life.

Stephen Coote, *John Keats: a life* (Hodder and Stoughton, 1995) focuses on Keats as a man of his time. It includes a comprehensive index.

Criticism

G. M. Matthews (ed.), *Keats: The Critical Heritage* (Routledge & Kegan Paul, 1971) is an impressive introduction to changing attitudes to Keats, exemplified by extracts of responses to Keats's writing between 1816 and 1863. It is now, unfortunately, out of print, but well worth chasing.

Brian Stone *Poetry of Keats* (Penguin, 1992) is an accessible introduction to Keats's life and work.

John Barnard, *John Keats* (Cambridge University Press, 1987) gives a detailed exploration of Keats's major poetry.

G. S. Fraser (ed.), *Keats: Odes* (Macmillan: Casebook Series, 1971) offers a selection of critical essays on Keats's odes.

John Spencer Hill (ed), *Keats: Narrative Poems* (Macmillan: Casebook Series, 1983) offers a selection of critical essays on Keats's narrative poems.

Marilyn Butler, *Romantics, Rebels and Reactionaries* (Oxford University Press, 1981) provides a detailed and useful discussion of English literature and its background from 1760–1830.

INDEX OF SOME TOPICS
IN THE LETTERS

INDEX OF TITLES AND FIRST LINES OF POEMS